Stalled Wheels of Justice

Advance Praise for the Book

'In Indian courts, the process is the punishment. This is an oft-repeated statement but remains theoretical for most. Unfortunately for many of our citizens, it is a lived reality. In *Stalled Wheels of Justice*, Shishir Tripathi tells the stories of Umakant Mishra, Machal Lalung, and several others to bring to life how delays in the judicial process have ruined lives and families. With detailed data that will be a valuable resource for researchers, Tripathi points out where the bottlenecks in the system are and what reforms are necessary. Ultimately, despite the stories of injustice it details, the book is a story of hope and resolve–of the work we, as citizens, must all put in to ensure that we have a justice system that delivers for the poorest, most destitute, and most needy citizen, who comes knocking at its doors.'

Arghya Sengupta

Research director, Vidhi Centre for Legal Policy

'Even though "Justice delayed is justice denied" is an old saying, the treatment of this pandemic disease in this book is contemporary. This is an excellent book that must find a place in everyone's library. It's a must-read for lawyers, law students, policymakers, judges, and the general readers.'

Vivek Sood

Senior advocate, Supreme Court of India

'The art of journalism is to make almost every specialised subject more relatable to the lay audience. This is all the more expected of the fourth estate when a particular subject, such as law and the legal system, has a direct bearing on access to justice for everyone. It is for this reason that quality legal journalism is indispensable for the health of a constitutional democracy that professes a commitment to the rule of law. Shishir Tripathi's book is a much-needed contribution in the direction of making the justice dispensation system more relatable and accessible to people who are the intended beneficiaries of the system but who, more often than not, do not benefit from it. In that sense, the book also holds a mirror to our institutions in the hope of lending the process of dispensing justice a human touch despite the need for objectivity. As for readability, Shishir's diverse experience in legal reportage shines through the book in the form of the real-world examples he has chosen to make his point, and the lucidity of presentation is consistent with his track record. I wish Shishir all the very best for the book and hope that it penetrates and impacts the halls and corridors of justice.'

J. Sai Deepak

Advocate, Supreme Court of India

Stalled Wheels of Justice

Shishir Tripathi

ink | OCCAM

ISBN: 978-81-967375-3-5

First published in India 2024
This edition published 2024

BluOne Ink Pvt. Ltd
A-76, 2nd Floor, Sector 136, Noida
Uttar Pradesh 201301
www.bluone.ink
publisher@bluone.ink

Printed and bound in India at Nutech Print Services - India

ink | OCCAM

Yaksha: What is heavier than the earth?
Yudhishthira: One's mother.
Yaksha: What is higher than the heavens?
Yudhishthira: One's father.

To
Papa and Maa

Contents

Foreword

Stalled Wheels of Justice records the malady as well as the remedy. It contains heartrending stories of litigants who were crushed under the wheels of justice. Mr Shishir Tripathi, the author of this book, has the unique advantage of hailing from a family of lawyers as well as being a journalist. Therefore, he has been able to provide an insight into the way in which judiciary in India functions, what ails the system of administration of justice in our country, the issue of access to justice, the way certain laws are misused, the performance of the Legal Services Authority over the years, the factors that contribute to the problem and 'The Alternative'.

The problem of backlog of cases in India and the attempts to tackle the same is a century old. It is rather a matter of coincidence that this book is being released exactly after 100 years of the constitution of the first committee to examine the problem of delay.

The first committee to examine the problem of delay was set up in 1924 under Justice Rankin. Since then, several committees have put forth recommendations, but little progress has been made on the implementation front. These include the Justice S.R. Das High Court Committee (1949), the Trevor Harris Committee in West Bengal (1949), the Wanchoo Committee in Uttar Pradesh (1950), Justice J.C. Shah Committee (1972), Satish Chandra Committee (1986), and the First Malimath Committee (1990).

Apart from these, the Law Commission has addressed the issue in several reports since 1955: the 14th, 79th, 80th, 120th, 121st, and 124th reports. Other reports on this issue such as 221st, 222nd, and, especially, the 229th touched upon the issue of delay, pendency, and arrears. The Second Malimath Committee submitted its recommendations in 2003. In the Conferences of Chief Justices and Chief Ministers, the issue of backlog has always been a hot topic. On 24–25 October 2009, judges of higher courts, officials of the Ministry of Law and Justice, members of Bar Council of India, and the faculty of the Indian Law Institute and other academic institutions gathered for the 'National Consultation for Strengthening the Judiciary Towards Reducing Pendency and Delays' and came up with suggestions. The amendments to the Civil Procedure Code in the year 1999/2002 giving a big push for Alternative Dispute Resolution (ADR) also attempted to remove the logjam.

Unfortunately, the reports, recommendations, and consultation papers just piled up without any concrete result being achieved. This is perhaps due to the fact, in my opinion, that all the reports and recommendations attempted to provide only a symptomatic relief to the ailment as allopathic medicines do to the common cold.

There appears to be a failure on the part of all the committees to understand the litigation culture of the common man in the country. The way the psyche of a litigant in this country works is very peculiar. While 50 per cent of the people who come to the court or are dragged into the court want speedy justice. The other 50 per cent appear to come to court not with the objective of securing a justified victory but with an object of prolonging the status quo, thereby retaining an unjust enrichment or an undeserved advantage. In a litigation between a landlord and a tenant, the tenant merely wants prolongation of the proceedings. So is the case of a borrower in a litigation between a lender and a borrower. In this tug of war between those who want speedy justice and those who want justice delayed, the court is caught.

Many bystanders jump to their feet and suggest that courts should be ruthless in dealing with defaulters including borrowers, tenants, etc., so that they do not achieve the object of delaying justice. But the solution is not as simple as that. In a country where capital is scarce and ownership of land, buildings, and houses is in the hands of a miniscule minority, making all others depend upon such a minority for locating their homes and establishments (small, medium, or big), the pace with which the wheels of justice can move is controlled by the other 50 per cent of the litigants.

I think the solutions suggested by many of the committees in the past replicated developed societies' committees' recommendations. In developed societies, the cost of litigation is prohibitively high. Keeping the cost of litigation high is antithetical to the idea of access to justice. A high cost of litigation will deter litigation and keep the idea of access to justice illusory.

All scholars and analysts invariably commit two mistakes while addressing the problem of backlog of cases. One is that they do not try to find out why a large number of people keep coming to courts despite their abject failure to dispense justice. The other is that no worthwhile research is done to find out how many cases get disposed of within a reasonable period of time. What makes news is only failure and not stories of success.

Therefore, I hope that Shishir Tripathi's book becomes an eye-opener for more and more research in this area.

I congratulate him for providing a gripping narrative, maintaining a good tempo, and providing a lot of statistics. The success of a book depends predominantly on its utility value for students and scholars alike and the style of writing. Shishir Tripathi has succeeded in both. I wish him success in all his future endeavours.

26 January 2024

Justice V. Ramasubramanian
Former Judge, Supreme Court of India

Acknowledgements

First and foremost, I would like to thank Mr Ajay Singh, who has been a constant motivation for me and someone I look up to. During my stint at *GovernanceNow* and Firstpost, he gave me ample opportunities to experiment, explore, and experience various forms of writing–from short blogs to lengthy field reports and from analyses to features. This book is a result of the confidence that he instilled in me as a young reporter and writer. He is the best editor and guide I could have asked for.

To Mr Ashish Mehta, the most gentle and affable person around. He is the most amazing bibliophile and repository of immense knowledge yet a completely unassuming person, a fact that makes him so different from the multitude. I will always be grateful for his mentorship.

Every book is an idea that needs a kindling. For this book, it came from Mr Utpal Kumar, an elder brother, mentor, and guide. His continuous nudge is what made me believe that the idea is workable as a book and the fact that I can write it. There were occasions when self-doubt popped in. On such occasions, I reached out to him for a dose of assurance, and he was there always.

To Mr J Sai Deepak, who needs no introduction, for his continuous support. His life is an inspiration to me, and he has always been there for guidance despite his crazy schedule.

My publisher, Mr Praveen Tiwari, whose instant approval for the book instilled confidence in me that I am on the right path. His calm and gentle demeanour assured me that I could not find a better person to guide me through this journey. Special thanks to Thanglenhao Haokip, senior editor at BluOne Ink, for managing the editing process brilliantly; he made the book look good.

A very special thanks to Dr Arghya Sengupta, research director, Vidhi Centre Legal Policy, who is a brilliant legal mind and whose writings have been a reference point for many of my write-ups. I am grateful that he took time from his busy schedule to read the early draft of the book and shared his feedback generously.

A special mention to Mr Vivek Sood, senior advocate, Supreme Court of India, who is also a prolific writer. I would like to express my sincere gratitude to him for his advance review and encouragement.

Samarpan Vashishtha, my younger brother, is a partner in crime and whom I can affably call my research assistant. Without his support, this book would not have been possible.

To my teacher for life and mentor Mrs Shubhra Ranjan for her endearing presence and all her encouragement.

Last but not the least, a special thanks to those special people who keep me moving, filling my life with light and joy, happiness and contentment.

My wife, Pragati, whose love is the driving force of my life and whose warmth sustains me; she nourishes and believes in my dreams more dearly than I would ever do.

Aadya, my daughter, who fills me with energy and hope for a better future.

My elder brother, Mr Rishi Tripathi, whose zest for life and perseverance in all his pursuits I try to imbibe. To his family—bhabhi and the two children—who are an absolute bundle of joy.

To the parents of my wife, who gave me much more than my 'better half'—my 'best half'.

To Jaya, Ashish, Vivek, and Pooja for being the source of joy and laughter.

To Vibhava Prakash Tripathi, my Fufaji; Shalini Tripathi, my bua; and her two wonderful daughters, Ruchi and Ananya, for all their love.

To Yogesh Rajput, Abhimanyu Singh, and Arun Tiwari, three of my dearest friends who always believe in me.

To Nishant Yadav, Vishal Srivastava, and Pankaj Kumar, my elder brothers from different mothers, your mere presence is extremely reassuring.

To Chitleen Sethi, an elder sister whose company is a source of joy. From her, I learnt to be unapologetically myself—to be affectionate, kind, and humble.

If mentions are expressions of gratitude, the absence of any name is just a chance. I will be eternally grateful to all those who in some or another way helped me become what I am.

Prologue

'Let the law take its course' is an often-used axiom in the legal world. The expression is used with a tone of authority and finality because it is assumed that the law will take the right course and justice will be served. But does that always happen? It is a question which has a disappointing answer.

In the legal labyrinth, one has to often struggle for years, sometimes decades, to find an exit. In many cases, at the end of the long tunnel what one encounters is engulfing darkness and the light remains elusive. The wheels of justice are stalled, and when they move, they move at their own pace.

If there can be a face for the stalled wheels of justice, it would be Machal Lalung. In July 2005, Lalung walked free after fifty-four years as an undertrial. He languished in the Lokpriya Gopinath Bordoloi Mental Hospital in Tezpur for thirty-eight years, even after being declared fit by the hospital in 1967.

'I don't know why I was arrested nor do I remember the date. I was then a young boy like him,' said Lalung, pointing to his college-going grand-nephew.[1]

Machal Lalung was arrested when he was 23 years old in 1951 under Section 326 of the Indian Penal Code (IPC) for voluntarily causing grievous injuries. Ironically, his case never came up for hearing even once.[2] As he was found mentally unstable, he was sent for treatment and then forgotten.

When Lalung was released, he was 77 years old. When the story was published, a Supreme Court lawyer wrote a letter to the then chief justice of India highlighting Lalung's plight. The chief justice of India took cognisance of it and eventually framed guidelines for undertrials who are languishing either in jails or mental hospitals for longer periods. Lalung was awarded compensation.

But what can compensate for an entire life spent behind the bars?

Attributing the quote to Pip—the hero of Charles Dickens's novel *Great Expectations*, Amartya Sen in *An Idea of Justice* writes, 'In the little world in which children have their existence there is nothing so finely perceived and finely felt, as injustice.'

Sen adds, 'But the strong perception of manifest injustice applies to adult human beings as well. What moves us, reasonably enough, is not the realisation that the world falls short of being completely just—which few of us expect—but that there are clearly remediable injustices around us which we want to eliminate.'

What comes closest to this idea of manifest injustice is 'justice delayed' and unequal access to justice.

The story of Machal Lalung is not an exception or aberration. There are numerous Lalungs for whom the wheels of justice are stalled and when they move, they move at a very slow pace.

Chapter 1, 'Justice Delayed, Denied', chronicles the stories of people for whom justice remained a distant dream, and in the cases where and when it was served, it was too late. It chronicles the story of a father who fought for his murdered son for three decades, only to lose both the battles—of life and that of justice. It tells the story of a humble government employee whose entire life was destroyed for ten paise. It tells the story of Nikhil Chandra Mondal and Guna Mahto, who had to give four decades of their lives to finally get what can be technically called judgment but not 'justice'.

A society, no matter how materially developed and advanced, will cease to exist if justice is not the order of the day. Any system of thought, any institution, or any arrangement must be rejected and revised if it is unjust. Each person possesses an inviolability founded on justice, but what to do when justice is not only expensive, evasive, and elusive but also out of bounds from the reach of an ordinary citizen?

Justice has been a primary concern of political philosophy. It is the architectonic and overarching construct around which different theories, ranging from that of the state to rights and freedom, revolve. From Plato to John Rawls, Amartya Sen to Michael J. Sandel, philosophers and theorists have pondered over the question of justice.

Justice is considered the first virtue of social institutions. John Rawls rightly puts it as 'Justice is the first virtue of social institutions, as truth is of systems of thought. A theory, however elegant and economical, must be rejected or revised if it is untrue; likewise laws and institutions no matter how efficient and well-arranged must be reformed or abolished if they are unjust.'

Political theorists make a distinction between procedural and substantive justice, which is of utmost importance in the context of the theme of this book. Procedural justice is primarily concerned with the 'justness' of the procedure, whereas those batting for substantive justice want the outcome to be 'just' as well. Norman P. Barry in *Introduction to Modern Political Theory* writes, 'Procedural justice is exemplified in competitions, such as races. A fair race is not one in which the person who wins morally deserves to win but one in which there is no cheating, nobody jumps the guns or has an unfair advantage through the use of drugs'. The problem with proponents of procedural justice is that they fail to take into account those external factors that largely influence the outcome. Despite the fair rule, there might be athletes in racing who might have an advantage over others given their social and economic background–advantages that can be expressed in terms of better training facilities and diet.

Corresponding to this idea of procedural and substantive justice is the idea of 'procedure established by law' and 'due process of law'. During the framing of the Indian Constitution, there was vigorous debate around the usage of these two terms. On the one hand, the procedure established by law connotes that any outcome in the form of a law is to be held valid if it has followed the correct procedure for its enactment. On the other hand, due process of law calls for the fairness of the outcome, not limiting itself to adherence to the rule to reach that outcome.

Initially, when Jawaharlal Nehru introduced the objective resolution in the Constituent Assembly in December 1946, which was meant to chart out the guiding principles for the framers of the Constitution, it faced harsh criticisms from Dr B.R. Ambedkar, who was the chairperson of the drafting committee.

Dr Ambedkar said, 'I find that this part of the Resolution, although it enunciates certain rights, does not speak of remedies. All of us are aware of the fact that rights are nothing unless remedies are provided whereby people can seek to obtain redress when rights are invaded. I find a complete absence of remedies. Even the usual formula, that no man's life, liberty and property shall be taken without the due process of law, finds no place in the Resolution'.[3]

While the due process clause could not be included in the objective resolution, it did find a place in the basic draft that Benegal Narsing Rau, the constitutional advisor to the Constituent Assembly, had prepared for its members. Clause 16 of Rau's basic draft reads, 'No person shall be deprived of his life or personal liberty without due process of law'. However, due process was omitted and replaced by the procedure established by law in the final draft by an interesting turn of events.

After submitting the final draft, Rau left on his foreign tour. During his sojourn, he met Justice Felix Frankfurter of the U.S. Supreme Court, with whom he shared the basic draft and who, in turn, advised him to refrain from using the phrase 'by due process of law' as it would 'embolden Indian judges to indiscriminately invalidate economic and welfare laws, duly enacted by the people's representatives, for violating an individual's liberty,' writes Vikram Raghavan in his article titled The Curious Case of 'Due Process' in the Indian Constitution published in *The Indian Forum*.[4]

Raghavan adds, 'Rau returned to New Delhi in early December 1947. In a report to the assembly's president, Rau highlighted Frankfurter's belief that a due-process guarantee was undemocratic. Frankfurter felt that due process would enable judges to veto laws validly enacted by the people's representatives.' The draft constitution, which the committee finalised in February 1948, omitted any reference to due process. Draft Article 15 was the functional equivalent of Clause 16 in Rau's draft. It declared, 'No person shall be deprived of his life or personal liberty except according to procedure established by law'.

While the due process lost the battle in the Constituent Assembly, it made a comeback three decades later with the Maneka Gandhi case. The case was related to the impounding of Maneka Gandhi's passport, who was the daughter-in-law of former prime minister Indira Gandhi. In 1977, Indira Gandhi was defeated in the elections held after the national emergency was revoked. The Janta government came into power. Maneka Gandhi had to travel abroad during that time. However, she received a communication that her passport was impounded in 'public interest' under the relevant section of the Passports Act. On receiving the communication, she sought to clarify the reasons behind the action, but her request was turned down. Following this, she filed a writ petition in the Supreme Court challenging the order to impound her passport.

This was a 'small case' but resulted in a 'large judgment'. The case marked the reincarnation of the due process clause. Although the makers of the Constitution rejected the American due process clause, the Supreme Court's judgment in Maneka Gandhi effectively meant that 'procedure' established by law, under Article 21, interpreted according to Maneka Gandhi, would read as 'No person shall be deprived of his life and personal liberty except according to *fair, just and reasonable* procedure established by v*alid law*'.[5]

Until Maneka Gandhi's judgment, 'the view which prevailed in our Supreme Court was that there was no guarantee in our Constitution against arbitrary legislation upon personal liberty. Hence, if a competent legislature makes a law providing that a person may be deprived of his liberty in certain circumstances and in a certain manner, the validity of the law could not be challenged in a court of law on the ground that the law is unreasonable, unfair and unjust'.[6]

However, in Maneka Gandhi's case, it was held that a law coming under Article 21 must also satisfy the requirements of Article 19. In other words, a law made by the State that seeks to deprive a person of their liberty must prescribe a procedure for such deprivation, which must not be arbitrary, unfair, or unreasonable.[7]

The introduction of the due process clause through the Menaka Gandhi case 'empowered the courts to expand the limited phraseology of the right to life under the Constitution, to include a wide range of un-enumerated rights'.[8] Deriving from Article 21, among various rights, is the right to a fair and speedy trial.

Another idea relevant to the debate around law and justice is that of *niti* and *nyaya*. Amartya Sen in his book *The Idea of Justice* provides a distinction between nyaya and niti. Whereas niti deals with just rules and institutions, nyaya is about their realisation. 'One example of some interest and relevance is an important distinction between two different concepts of justice in early Indian jurisprudence—between niti and nyaya. The former idea, that of niti, relates to organizational propriety as well as behavioural correctness, whereas the latter, nyaya, is concerned with what emerges and how, and in particular, the lives that people are actually able to lead. The distinction, the relevance of which will be discussed in the Introduction, helps us to see clearly that there are two rather different, though not unrelated, kinds of justness for which the idea of justice has to cater,' writes Sen.

The inherent idea in the substantive theory of justice, due process clause, and the notion of nyaya different from niti is that of fairness. The underlying proposition behind it is aptly expressed in the dictum that was laid down by the then lord chief justice of England, Lord Hewart in the case of *Rex vs Sussex Justices*. It reads, 'It is not merely of some importance, but it is of fundamental importance that, justice should not only be done but should manifestly and undoubtedly be seen to be done'.

Indeed, justice should manifestly and undoubtedly be seen to be done and to ensure this, the outcome should be seen to be fair. However, when someone has to wait for justice for years and decades, it is a miscarriage of justice not only in substantive terms but in procedural sense too. Procedures for delivering justice can be so taxing and arduous that the whole meaning and the very essence of justice are rendered meaningless.

In *Vakil Prasad Singh vs the State of Bihar*, the Supreme Court made some important observations that are of great importance in the current context. It said, 'Time and again this Court has emphasised the need for speedy investigations and trial as both are mandated by the letter and spirit of the provisions of the CrPC (in particular, Sections 197, 173, 309, 437 (6) and 468, etc.) and the constitutional protection enshrined in Article 21 of the Constitution. Inspired by the broad sweep and content of Article 21 as interpreted by a seven-judge Bench of this Court in *Maneka Gandhi vs Union of India & Anr*, in *Hussainara Khatoon & Ors vs Home Secretary, State of Bihar*, this Court had observed that Article 21 confers a fundamental right on every person not to be deprived of his life or liberty except according to procedure established by law; that such procedure is not some semblance of a procedure but the procedure should be "reasonable, fair, and just"; and therefrom flows, without doubt, the right to a speedy trial. It was also observed that no procedure which does not ensure a reasonably quick trial can be regarded as "reasonable, fair, or just" and it would fall foul of Article 21.' The court clarified that speedy trial means reasonably expeditious trial, which is an integral and essential part of the fundamental right to life and liberty enshrined in Article 21.

Hussainara Khatoon & Ors vs Home Secretary, State of Bihar, is a landmark case in which the apex court gave a wider interpretation of Article 21 and held that speedy trial is the fundamental right of every citizen and made important remarks worth reproducing here. It said, 'The State cannot avoid its constitutional obligation to provide speedy trial to the accused by pleading financial or administrative inability. The State is under a constitutional mandate to ensure speedy trial and whatever is necessary for this purpose has to be done by the State. It is also the constitutional obligation of this Court as the guardian of the fundamental rights of the people, as a sentinel on the qui vive, to enforce the fundamental right of the accused to speedy trial by issuing the necessary directions to the State which may include taking of positive action, such as augmenting and strengthening the investigative machinery, setting up new courts, building new courthouses, providing more staff and equipment to the courts, appointment of additional judges and other measures calculated to ensure speedy trial.'

Justice, to be fair, needs to be equally accessible to everyone and dispensed on time. The oft-quoted axiom 'justice delayed is justice denied' should be the touchstone of ascertaining the fairness of the justice delivery system.

Former chief justice of the U.S. Supreme Court, Warren Burger famously said, 'The notion that ordinary people want black-robed judges, well-dressed lawyers in fine courtrooms as settings to resolve their disputes is incorrect. People with problems, like people with pains, want relief and they want it as quickly and inexpensively as possible.'

Ironically, the wheels of justice move in a particular fashion. People often get 'judgment' and justice remains elusive.

Apart from the delay in dispensing justice, another important issue that bounds the wheels of justice is unequal access to justice. Years ago, Leeman Abbot, in relation to affluent America, had said, 'If ever a time shall come when in this city only the rich can enjoy law as a doubtful luxury, when the poor who need it most cannot have it, when only a golden key will unlock the door to the courtroom, the seeds of revolution will be sown, the fire-brand of revolution will be lighted and put into the hands of men and they will almost be justified in the revolution which will follow.'

The sense of relative deprivation in terms of unequal access to justice subdues the halo woven around the 'temples of justice'.

The former chief justice of India, N.V. Ramana, while speaking on this issue in March 2021, said, 'Ever since we declared ourselves to be an independent nation, we found ourselves caught between the twin problems of "poverty" and "access to justice". The architects of modern India have debated this issue on several national and international platforms. Sadly, even after 74 years of independence, we are still discussing the same issue.'[9]

Justice Ramana recounted how he had been approached by an elderly woman years ago while he was the chief justice of the Delhi High Court. She had asked him when he planned to put a cap on lawyers' fees so the poor could afford the best legal advice.

'I responded, "Madam, the court cannot control these things". She asked me, "Sir, tell me then how people like us can even come to the courts",' Justice Ramana narrated.

Beginning from filing a case to applying for protection from arrest, seeking bail, or the probability of getting a favourable judgment, all crucial steps of the legal tangle are influenced by the position and privilege enjoyed by one. Justice comes at a cost, and it tilts in favour of the privileged.

As discussed above, Chapter 1 focusses on the issue of inordinate delay in dispensing justice and the reasons behind it. While the judiciary is blamed for the delay, squarely blaming it is unjust. There are various factors behind the delay, which in many cases are beyond the control of the judiciary. The other branches of government are also responsible for that to some extent. And those reasons need to be examined and analysed.

Chapter 2 'Heavy Cost of Justice' delves into an important issue related to access to justice. The chapter tries to answer an important question: what is the cost of justice? Is it equal for those with big pockets and those living a life of mere subsistence? Backed by numerous studies and data, this chapter aims to show

how the cost of justice is too heavy to be borne by a common person and how the legal cost of a case leaves a heavy economic strain on a common man.

Misuse of law is the institutionalised miscarriage of justice. Certain laws like 'The Scheduled Castes and Scheduled Tribes (Prevention of Atrocities) Act', 1989, and Section 498A of the IPC were enacted to provide the required safeguards for vulnerable sections of society, but their misuse for settling personal scores while raising serious questions about its utility also dent its credibility. Chapter 3 'Misuse of Law, Travesty of Justice' tries to throw light on such laws.

One way of looking at the problem of delay and unequal access to justice is from the prism of demand and supply. The number of cases that need to be adjudicated is an example of the demand for justice and judicial infrastructure that includes human and material resources is an indicator of the supply. It is a known fact that demand for justice exceeds the supply and this mismatch between the two creates a disequilibrium that shifts the balance of justice in favour of those who have the resources to jump the queue. With 21 judges per million and the number of pending cases that run in crores, it does not take much to guess that justice cannot be dispensed equally.

While holding the judiciary accountable for delay and unequal access is important, it is equally needed to look into the roadblocks that are beyond the control of the judiciary. To a larger extent, the lack of proper judicial infrastructure in terms of both human and material resources should be an important point of focus in any analysis of the criminal justice delivery system.

According to the National Judicial Data Grid (NJDG), over 4.5 crore cases are pending in India's district and subordinate courts. Lack of proper infrastructure is one of the main reasons for this backlog. Infrastructure includes judges, auxiliary staff, courtrooms, and technological know-how to facilitate the judicial process. In the Union Budget for 2022-23, Rs 858 crore was allocated to develop judicial infrastructure. The Ministry of Law and Justice accounted only for 0.1 per cent of the Union budget. However, a positive development took place in 2023 when 7000 crore were provisioned for the launch of the third phase of the e-courts project in the Union Budget. This would certainly ensure 'Ease of Justice' and further improve the justice delivery system. Chapter 4 'Infrastructure Woes' dwells on the nitty-gritty of judicial infrastructure, the roadblocks, and the way out.

Right to legal counsel and adequate legal representation is the bedrock of a fair trial. The National Legal Services Authority (NALSA) has been constituted under the Legal Services Authorities Act, 1987 to provide free legal services to the weaker sections of society. But how far has this been able to fulfil its purpose is a question that needs to be probed. Chapter 5 'Right to Legal Aid' tries to answer this question.

Chapter 6 'Public Interest Litigation' discusses the role of PIL as an important mechanism in seeking justice for weaker sections of society apart from addressing important social, political, economic, and environmental issues. It also throws light on the fact that how its rampant misuse has dented its credibility.

The way out of the legal logjam is working on both sides: the demand and supply. Alternative Dispute Resolution (ADR) is one way of adding to the supply chain in the form of providing a mechanism of dispute resolution outside the court. Lok Adalats can play an important role in dispute resolution in the most inexpensive and effective manner. This has been dealt with in some detail in chapter 7 'The Hope: Alternative Dispute Redressal'.

This book is not a commentary on law; that has never been the intention behind this book. That is something best left to the jurists, lawyers, and constitutional experts. This is the story of law not being able to transform into justice. This is the story of a process that I witnessed as a court reporter—a process that former chief justice of India N V Ramana equated with 'punishment'.

Addressing the 18th All India Legal Service Authorities Meet at Jaipur in July 2022, Chief Justice Ramana said, 'In our criminal justice system, the process is the punishment. From hasty indiscriminate arrests to difficulty in obtaining bail, the process leading to the prolonged incarceration of undertrials needs urgent attention.'[10]

It is a fact that when the judicial process becomes the punishment, the justice-seekers become the first victims.

This is the story of the process and its victims.

CHAPTER 1

Justice Delayed, Denied

Tale of Two Judgments

In 2013, two separate trial courts in the country–one in Kanpur, Uttar Pradesh and another in Chandigarh–delivered their judgments in two different cases that were separated by geography but bound by their outcome. In both cases, judgments were delivered but justice looked evasive.

Both cases started their 'litigation journey' around three decades ago, in 1984 and 1985, respectively. In the first case, the 'accused' was alive to lament the wasted years, while in the second case, the petitioner died a year before the judgment came. The first case was of Umakant Mishra, a retired postman accused of siphoning 57 rupees and 60 paise out of a money order he was supposed to deliver.

The other case was related to the alleged murder of 21-year-old Inderjit Singh, which took place in 1984. Allah Singh, the father of the victim, died in 2012 at the age of 87 awaiting justice.

In the first case, it was the State that was fighting against the individual, making the tragedy one sided, given the government had all the means at its disposal to pursue the lengthy legal battle, and it was only Umakant Mishra who faced the brunt of a three-decade legal battle.

In the second case, apart from Allah Singh, the lives of the four accused, one of them a juvenile, were ruined. The burden of litigation—both financially and socially—destroyed the litigants.

For 29 years, Umakant Mishra lived with the tag of a thief, and in 2013 when the court of the metropolitan magistrate in Kanpur gave the judgment of not guilty, Mishra was already 65, retired from the postal department that took him to court, and had little reason to celebrate.

The acquittal had come at a price—he had spent almost thirty years of his life making rounds of court with lawyers provided by the state legal services authority. In the close-knit community he lived, the stigma of being a thief stuck. The court order did little to lighten that burden.

Umakant Mishra lived to see himself acquitted. But when a Special Central Bureau of Investigation (CBI) court in Chandigarh cleared four men of charges of murdering his son, there was no one from Allah Singh's family to hear the judgment.

Singh, who tirelessly fought to get justice for his son, had died a year before the judgment came. He was 87. Till then, he had not missed a single hearing, as people and lawyers recounted. Hoping for some closure, he would come prepared—food and water in his small bag.

The four accused, one of them not even 18 at the time of the incident, ended up spending the best years of their life in jail as the trial dragged on. Their families and that of Singh were drained of money, fighting the case in which there were no winners.

For Kawaljeet Singh, Inderjit's brother, the battle was half-lost when his father, who gave his life fighting for justice, died a year before the judgment came. 'After fighting for all these years, my father turned into a fragile old man with little reason to live. We always saw tears in his eyes. He used to say that he would fight for justice till his last breath,' Kawaljeet recounted.[1]

Having seen his grandfather wither day by day, Inderjit's nephew Iminder Singh said, 'I don't see any reason to continue this struggle. My grandfather struggled for almost three decades but died at the age of 87 as a helpless and broken man. We waited for almost twenty-eight years for justice, but it eluded us always.'[2]

Kawaljeet added, 'My younger brother was so full of life. He wanted to be an IAS officer. While working at Central Warehousing Corporation in Chandigarh, he was also preparing for various competitive exams.'[3]

Vinay Jhingan, a former public prosecutor in the case and counsel for Inderjit's father, said, 'I was so moved by the indomitable spirit of Allah Singh. After retiring from service, I became his lawyer. I remember he used to come thrice a week to court and spend the whole day there. His sole aim in life was to get justice for his son.'[4]

The ordeal was not limited to the family of Allah Singh. It severely affected the lives of the accused too, especially Khushwant Singh, who was 12 years old at the time of the incident. He was acquitted by the juvenile justice board in February 2014, but the entire process took a heavy toll on his life prospects.

In an interview with *The Hindustan Times*, Kushwant had said, 'I do not know how to react. Of course, the order proves my innocence but the cost I have paid is too high—my entire life.'[5]

Court battles in India are fought over many generations and when they come to an end, if at all, there is no winner. Lives are destroyed, careers and reputations lay in tatters, and finances are ruined. The battle for justice in India is not for the faint-hearted. Ironically, the poor and middle class are virtually priced out of a system that is meant to protect them. The system seems geared towards tiring out litigants and heavily tilted in favour of the moneyed.

Father's Legal Battle Made Son a Lawyer

K.K. Jerath was a chief engineer in Chandigarh in 1998 when eight cases were registered against him and several other people for alleged corruption. In the cases fought from 1998 to 2014, Jerath was acquitted in all eight of them. One case was clubbed with a similar case, and in the eighth case, the closure report was accepted by the court.

In 2014, while acquitting Jerath in the last pending case, the court, in its judgment, observed, 'There is no ring of truth in the prosecution version ... it would be quite unjustified to award the conviction on the basis of the testimonies of hostile witness.'

The judgment further added, 'This court fails to understand as to how the faith of common man can be commended for criminal justice if the investigation is found to be tainted, motivated, and defective. In the present case also, the Investigation Officer recorded the additional statements of the two approvers Jagdish Mitter and A.K. Sachdeva merely to inculpate the innocent persons for reasons best known to him.'

After Jerath was acquitted in all eight cases, the Chandigarh administration filed an appeal in the Punjab and Haryana High Court. Dismissing one such appeal in July 2015, filed by the Chandigarh Administration, Justice Rameshwar Singh Malik of Punjab and Haryana High Court said in its judgment, 'A bare perusal of the impugned judgment will show that the Special Judge, Chandigarh, has discussed, considered and appreciated each and every relevant aspect of the matter and that too very meticulously. All evidence, documentary as well as oral, brought on record has been considered in minute detail. On further scanning the testimony of prosecution witnesses, the trial court, in its analysis, found that the prosecution had failed to bring home the guilt against the accused persons.'

It added, 'The evidence brought on record was not found sufficient to record the conviction and the accused were acquitted of the charges framed against them. This court feels no hesitation to conclude that the trial court committed no error of law while passing the impugned judgment of acquittal, and the same deserves to be upheld.'

When Jerath was first arrested and jailed, his bank accounts and properties were seized, and he was reduced to the position of that of a common man-litigant who stares at a vacuum to understand how to fight for justice.

'See, I was falsely implicated in all these cases at the behest of then home secretary Anuradha Gupta. When I was arrested, my bank accounts were blocked and I could not use my own hard-earned money. For the initial year, I borrowed from my relatives and friends, but then I realised this was going to take long and started preparing myself to fight these cases on my own. I started arguing my cases on my own. In jail, I used to read IPC and CrPC and prepare my petitions. It was my son who became my assistant in this legal battle,' recalls Jerath.

Jerath's son Aushotosh, an engineer with a master's in management from IIM Bangalore, could not take up a regular job as he was busy supporting, assisting, and defending his father in his legal battle. The long journey of litigation that Aushotosh had to cover with his father acquainted him with the legal process so much that he studied law and is now a practising counsel in Punjab and Haryana High Court.

'I was just doing what any son would do. But when you ask me about the cost of litigation, I will tell you it has two sides. What we suffered is one thing. But just imagine that the Chandigarh administration spent crores, which obviously was taxpayers' money, in fighting these cases. They hired top criminal lawyers as special public prosecutors to ensure that my father was convicted.

They could have very well used this money to help those poor litigants who cannot afford lawyers,' said Aushotosh.

K.K. Jerath adds, 'I just feel that God was kind to me to give me enough strength to bear all this.'

Apart from Jerath, families of other 'accused' N.K. Gupta, R.P. Vashish, and K.K. Salgotra all have the same thing to say. The cost of litigation was those precious years of life that no one can bring back.

David and Goliath

Ranvir Singh Yadav worked as a conductor at Delhi Transport Corporation (DTC). In August 1973, he was accused by the checking staff of DTC on the allegation that he had collected 10 paise from a lady passenger against the actual fare of 15 paise and that he had pocketed the said amount by not issuing a ticket to her.

An inquiry was conducted against Yadav, and he was dismissed from service on 15 July 1976. Aggrieved by the dismissal order, Yadav raised an industrial dispute, and the matter was referred to the labour court. The labour court passed an order on 26 February 1990, holding inter alia that the inquiry conducted by DTC was illegal and unjustified. The court directed DTC to reinstate Yadav with full back wages.

Following this order, an appeal was made, and Yadav had to struggle for the next twenty-six years to get his dues. DTC challenged the verdict in the high court, which in 2008 dismissed its plea. DTC again moved the high court through the review petition, which was dismissed in 2016.

The state-run corporation informed the Delhi High Court that it had spent Rs 47,795 in pursuing litigation against a former conductor for charging 5 paise less for a ticket forty-one years ago.

When the high court finally dismissed the petition of DTC, it asked the transport body to pay Rs 30,000 to Mr Yadav. A gratuity of Rs 1.28 lakh and another Rs 1.37 lakh as central provident fund should be paid to him, it said. What the court said in a judgment was striking. The judgment read,

> The present petition plays out a modern-day version of the Biblical story of 'David and Goliath', where the petitioner/DTC, a public sector undertaking, has played to the hilt, the role of the giant, Goliath, a nine-foot soldier from Gath, who had vainly boasted that he could beat any individual soldier in the Israelite army and the respondent No. 3, who was employed as a conductor with the petitioner/DTC, is the contextual David, the shepherd boy, who has been valiantly facing the wrath of a leviathan in the shape of the petitioner/DTC, for the past over four decades, on an allegation that he had misappropriated 10 paise from a passenger without issuing her a ticket for an actual fare of 15 paise.

It added,

> Here is a case where the respondent No. 3/Workman has been fighting a prolonged battle with the petitioner/DTC spanning over 40 years and after having won the case before the labour court and the high court, he has not been able to reap the fruits. It is ironic that respondent No. 3 has by now reached the ripe old age of 73 years in litigation that had commenced in the year 1973 when he was all of 31 years old.

Fifty-Four Years to Decide a Land Dispute

In August 1967, Banaras Sah, a resident of Sitamarhi, Bihar, filed a plea in the trial court claiming ownership of six kathas of land against Krishna Kant Prasad. He also sought the conversion of the disputed land into its original state after the removal of any new construction over it.

The plaint was amended from time to time as the original plaintiff and defendants died in the course of a legal fight that lasted fifty-four years. The case dragged on for nineteen years in the trial court, which on 31 May 1986 dismissed the title suit of the plaintiffs primarily for the reason that the plaintiffs had failed to establish their title to the suit land and, hence, they were not entitled to evict Krishna Kant Prasad. Sahs appealed against the trial court's decision before the additional district judge Sitamarhi, who, on 7 December 1988, reversed the trial court order.

Following this, the legal heirs of Krishna Kant Prasad moved to the Patna High Court, where the single judge dismissed the appeal on 25 May 1989. Legal heirs of Krishna Kant Prasad thereupon filed a special leave petition in the Supreme Court. The Supreme Court took eleven years to deliver its judgment which was in favour of Krishna Kant Prasad.

In the judgment delivered on 23 February 2000, the apex court remanded the matter back to the high court for de novo consideration owing to the intricacies of land law involved in the case. Taking nine years to deliver its judgment, in August 2009, the single judge of the Patna High Court dismissed the appeal of Krishna Kant Prasad. After which, an appeal was again filed in the Supreme Court.

It was after fourteen years, a bench of Justice A.M. Khanwilkar and Justice Sanjiv Khanna, on 7 September 2021, brought to an end this half-century-old case when it passed an order in favour of Krishna Kant Prasad's heirs. While delivering the judgment, the Supreme Court, in great detail, dwelt upon the issue of pendency and delays in delivering justice.

Long Wait for Justice for Nikhil Chandra Mondal and Guna Mahto

In March 2023, in two different cases, the Supreme Court acquitted two men from the charges of murdering their wives.

In the first case, Nikhil Chandra Mondal was convicted by the high court for the murder of his wife, which took place on 11 March 1983, in the Burdwan district of West Bengal. Mondal was initially acquitted by the trial court in March 1987. But was later convicted by the high court on 15 December 2008.

However, the Supreme Court set aside the high court order convicting Mondal, ruling that his conviction was based on extra-judicial confessions, which cannot be sustained as it is a weak piece of evidence.

In the second case, the conviction of a man named Guna Mahto was set aside by the apex court. Mahto, a resident of erstwhile Daltonganj, was accused of murdering his wife, Deomatiya Devi, which took place in August 1988. Mahto was charged with the murder of his wife, and the trial court in May 2001, that is twelve years after the incident took place, convicted him of the murder. Following the conviction by the trial court, an appeal was made in the high court, which delivered its judgment in July 2004, wherein it affirmed the trial court judgment. Then, the case finally reached the apex court, which held Mahto not guilty in 2023.

This led the court to opine that the circumstances linking the accused to the crime were not proven at all.

'The courts below presumptively proceeded with the acquired assumption of the guilt of the accused for the reason that he was lastly seen with the deceased and lodged a false report, forgetting that as per the version of the father of the deceased, the father of the accused had himself apprised him of his missing daughter, at least two days prior to the incident. Doubt and suspicion cannot form the basis of guilt of the accused. The circumstances linking the accused to the crime are not proven at all, much less beyond reasonable doubt.' The Supreme Court, in its judgment, further said, 'In our considered view, the courts below have seriously erred in passing the order of conviction based on the incorrect and incomplete appreciation of evidence, causing serious prejudice to the accused, also resulting into a travesty of justice.'

Allah Singh and Guna Mahto are not aberrations, they are just hidden in the din of larger and 'more significant' constitutional debates. These are the people who are reduced to insignificant cogs in the wheels of justice. But they exist at all times. They face the grind of the judicial process, and they never cease to exist.

According to the National Judicial Data Grid, a total of 44,703,932 cases are pending before the different courts in India. Of this 33,726,601 are criminal cases and 10,977,331 are civil cases. Of these pending criminal cases, 97 per cent are more than one year old. Cases that are pending for more than 10 years total 3,230,452. Cases more than 20 years to 30 years old total 495,257. Cases pending for more than 30 years total 93,220.

By some estimates, that might look like an exaggerated extrapolation, it would take hundreds of years to clear this backlog. Noting that 'the sheer volume of pendency ... is creating an impediment,' Supreme Court judge Justice Sanjay Kishan Kaul warned that 'if every case has to be tried till the end, if every first appeal has to be heard by the courts, if every matter transcends itself into coming to the Supreme Court, 200 years, 500 years will also not see the end of this litigation'.[6]

According to one of the estimates by the Law Commission, it would require 464 years to clear the arrears with the present strength of judges. A 2018 paper by NITI Aayog said it would take more than 324 years to clear the backlogs.

Classic Case and Mirror to Frustrating Judicial Process

In what could be said as a case of self-reflection, the Supreme Court in October 2023 delivered judgment in a civil appeal in which the litigating started in the trial court in 1982 and dragged on for forty-one years. The apex court in the judgment said,

> Even after 41 years, the parties to this are still groping in the dark and litigating as to who should be brought on record as legal representative of the sole plaintiff Mrs Urmila Devi ... This is a classic case and a mirror to the fact that the litigant public may become disillusioned with judicial processes due to inordinate delay in the legal proceedings, not reaching its logical end, and moving at a snail's pace due to dilatory tactics adopted by one or the other party.

The apex court also listed cases that have been pending for more than fifty years. The three oldest civil and criminal cases were:

Top pending civil cases

1. West Bengal

(a) Civil Judge Senior Division, Malda – Partition Suit No.30 of 1952 – registered on 4 April 1952

(b) Civil Judge, Sr. Division, Medinipur – Other Suit No. 39 of 2017 registered on 15 September 1953

Top three pending criminal cases

(1) Maharashtra

(a) Chief Judicial Magistrate, Amravati – R.C.C. No. 2319 of 1959 – registered on 11 April 1959

(b) CJJD & JMFC Mehkar – R.C.C. No. 61 of 1960 – registered on 06 October 1959

(c) Chief Judicial Magistrate, Amravati – R.C.C.No.778 of 1961 – registered on 30 August 1961

The anguish of the apex court was palpable as it went on to underline the factors behind the judicial delays:

> 'The causes of delay are numerous loopholes in the law itself, redundant and voluminous paperwork, absence of the witnesses, adjournments sought and granted for no justifiable reason as also delay in service of summons, lack of implementation of the provisions of Code of Civil Procedure (hereinafter referred to as 'CPC') and Code of Criminal Procedure (hereinafter referred to as 'CrPC'), as the case may be. These are only illustrative and not exhaustive.

The court issued certain directions to expedite the judicial process:

i. All courts at district and taluka levels shall ensure proper execution of the summons and in a time-bound manner as prescribed under Order V Rule (2) of CPC and the same shall be monitored by principal district judges and after collating the statistics, they shall forward the same to be placed before the committee constituted by the high court for its consideration and monitoring.
ii. All courts at the district and taluka levels shall ensure that written statement is filed within the prescribed limit, namely as prescribed under Order VIII Rule (1) and preferably within thirty days, and to assign reasons in writing as to why the time limit is being extended beyond thirty days as indicated under proviso to sub-rule (1) of Order VIII of CPC.
iii. All courts at the district and taluka levels shall ensure after the pleadings are complete, the parties should be called upon to appear on the day fixed as indicated in Order X. The courts then shall record the admissions and denials and direct the parties to the suit to opt for either mode of the settlement outside the court as specified in Sub-section (1) of Section 89. The parties shall be given the option to fix the date of appearance before such forum or authority and in the event of the parties opting to any one of the modes

of settlement directions be issued to appear on the date, time, and venue fixed. The parties shall so appear before such authority/forum without any further notice at such designated place and time. It shall also be made clear in the reference order that the trial is fixed beyond the period of two months making it clear that in the event of Alternative Dispute Resolution (ADR) not being fruitful, the trial would commence on the next day so fixed and would proceed on a day-to-day basis.

iv. In the event of the party's failure to opt for ADR, namely resolution of the dispute as prescribed under Section 89 (1), the court should frame the issues for its determination within one week, preferably in the open court.

v. Fixing the date of trial shall be in consultation with the learned advocates appearing for the parties to enable them to adjust their calendars. Once the date of the trial is fixed, the trial should proceed accordingly to the extent possible on a day-to-day basis.

vi. Learned trial judges of district and taluka courts shall as far as possible maintain the diary to ensure that only such number of cases can be handled on any given day for trial and complete the recording of evidence to avoid overcrowding of the cases and as a sequence of it would result in adjournment being sought and thereby preventing any inconvenience being caused to the stakeholders.

vii. The counsels representing the parties may be enlightened of the provisions of Order XI and Order XII to narrow down the scope of dispute and it would also be the onerous responsibility of the Bar Associations and Bar Councils to have periodical refresher courses, preferably by virtual mode.

viii. The trial courts shall scrupulously, meticulously, and without fail comply with the provisions of Rule 1 of Order

XVII and once the trial has commenced, it shall proceed from day to day as contemplated under the proviso to Rule (2).

ix. The courts shall give meaningful effect to the provisions for payment of cost for ensuring that no adjournment is sought for procrastination of the litigation and the opposite party is suitably compensated if such adjournment is being granted.

x. After the trial, the oral arguments shall be heard immediately and continuously and judgment be pronounced within the period stipulated under Order XX of CPC.

xi. The statistics relating to the cases pending in each court beyond five years shall be forwarded by every presiding officer to the Principal District Judge once a month, who (Principal District Judge/District Judge) shall collate the same and forward it to the review committee constituted by the respective high courts for enabling it to take further steps.

xii. The committee so constituted by the hon'ble chief justice of the respective states shall meet at least once in two months and direct such corrective measures to be taken by the concerned court as deemed fit and shall also monitor the old cases (preferably which are pending for more than five years) constantly.

In a civil case, the Supreme Court went to length to discuss the issue of judicial delays and pendency. The amicus curiae gave details of how the case proceeded in the trial court by reproducing the entire order sheet. The order sheet was included in the judgment to show how a case moves at a snail's pace. And it is important to note here that the original litigation and the appeal commenced in 1977. Here is the order sheet from the second litigation that started in 1992.

A look at the progress of the case over the years would be instructive as it is the best evidence to show how a case is delayed for reasons that are well within the control of institutions that are part of the justice delivery system and are tasked with ensuring justice on time, without delay to those who knock its doors.

28 Feb 1992	Fresh summons to Defendants 1 and 2. Defendant 3 refused service. Proceeded ex-parte.
30 Mar 1992	Time sought to file a written statement for all the defendants. Allowed.
20 Apr 1992	Written statement filed. Fixed on 30.04.1992 for replication, admission/denial, and framing of issues.
01 May 1992	The plaintiff sought time to file replication.
11 May 1992	Replication filed. Adjourned for admission/denial on joint request.
17 Jul 1992	Arguments were heard on a preliminary issue.
20 Jul 1992	Suit stayed. The plaintiff was granted liberty to make an application for revival after disposal of RFA (OS) 4/82.
01 Jun 2001	The file was sent to the district judge for transferring the case to the proper court.
04 Jun 2001	District judge marked the case to the court of Shri Naipal Singh, Additional District Judge.
02 Jul 2001	The presiding officer is on leave. Fixed for 03.07.2001.
03 Jul 2001	A miscellaneous application notice was issued to the respondent. Main suit 47/92.
23 Aug 2001	A suit file be summoned. Notice of application to defendant.
16 Oct 2001	Copy of application given to all the defendants. Adjourned for reply to application and further proceedings.

05 Dec 2001	The suit has to proceed for the decision on merits.
28 Feb 2002	Application under Order 6 Rule 17 moved by defendant for amendment of written statement. Adjourned for reply and arguments on the application.
16 Apr 2002	As the value of the suit is below Rs 3 lakh, the suit is transferred to the court of civil judge.
23 Apr 2002	Reply to an application filed. Summons to defendants other than Defendant 3.
21 Aug 2002	Counsel for the parties not present.
28 Nov 2002	The presiding officer is on leave.
07 Dec 2002	At joint request, adjourned. Last opportunity.
22 Sep 2003	None present. Adjourned for arguments on Order 6 Rule 17. The file was transferred to the court of Shri Prashant Kumar, Civil Judge.
12 Nov 2003	The son of the plaintiff stated that the plaintiff has expired. Adjourned.
06 Dec 2003	The presiding officer is not available.
16 Jan 2004	Reply not filed. Counsel for the defendant seeks time to file a reply.
01 Mar 2004	Reply filed. Counsel for the defendant objected that the addresses of legal representatives were not correct.
24 Mar 2004	Application Order 22 Rule 3 is allowed. The right to sue survives. Order 6 Rule 17 pending for disposal.
27 Apr 2004	Arguments heard.
22 May 2004	The plaintiff wants to file written submissions with regard to clarification. Allowed.
03 Jul 2004	None for defendants. Written submissions filed by plaintiff.
28 Jul 2004	Present none. Order 6 Rule 17 dismissed.

02 Sep 2004 to 06 Oct 2004	None for Defendants. Fixed for preliminary enquiry.
28 Sep 2004	The defendant moved application Order 14 Rule 5. Notice issued.
06 Oct 2004	Issues reframed. The defendant sought time to cross-examine prosecution witness.
22 Nov 2004	Prosecution witness present. Defendant prayed for an adjournment. The defendant moved an application for transfer of the case. Last opportunity for cross-examination.
21 Dec 2004	Prosecution witness present. The previous cost was not pressed for. Prosecution witness sought time to obtain copies of documents.
10 Feb 2005	Prosecution witness cross-examined. Preliminary enquiry closed.
15 Mar 2005	No defence witness present
19 Apr 2005	Affidavit of defence witness filed. However, defence witness stated that he is not feeling well. Adjourned.
28 May 2004	The defendant stated that he does not want to lead evidence. Defence evidence closed. Fixed for final arguments.
15 Jul 2005	Stay by the high court in CM (Main) 1490/2005.
18 Jul 2005	Counsel for the defendant states that the high court has stayed the matter. Directed to file a copy of the order.
25 Aug 2005	No copy of the order is filed.
29 Oct 2005	Matter under stay by the high court.
30 Jan 2006	Fresh suit received by transfer. Adjourned for proper orders.
02 May 2006	Notice to defendants.
31 May 2006	Counsel for the defendants served but none appeared. Adjourned for final arguments.

21 Aug 2006	The file is not traceable. Adjourned.
09 Dec 2006	Present: Counsel for the plaintiff. Adjourned for final arguments.
19 Feb 2007	Counsel for the plaintiff. The proceedings were stayed by the high court.
21 Aug 2007	Counsel for the Plaintiff. The matter is under stay by the high court.
17 Dec 2007	CM (Main) 1490/2005 was dismissed by the high court. Stay vacated.
10 Jan 2008	Counsel for the plaintiff. None for the defendant. Adjourned.
12 Feb 2008	Defendant filed application O18 R17A. Copy supplied. Adjourned for reply and arguments.
30 Apr 2008	Reply filed by the plaintiff. Application allowed to cost of Rs 7000, out of which Rs 1000 to be deposited in legal aid. Adjourned for DE.
31 Jul 2008	The defendant sought adjournment on the grounds that the witness was not feeling well.
29 Sep 2008	The plaintiff moved application Order 6 Rule 17. Copy supplied.
23 Dec 2008	Reply filed. Come up with arguments on the application
21 May 2009	Part arguments heard.
22 Jul 2009	The plaintiff does not press for the application. Dismissed. To come up for defence evidence.
05 Oct 2009	The defendants witness was not present. Application for exemption allowed. Affidavit already filed.
23 Oct 2009	Application under Order 7 Rule 1 CPC filed. Dismissed. Affidavit of Kishan Gopal tendered as defence witness 1, and he is cross-examined and discharged. No other witness. Defence evidence closed.

11 Jan 2010	The presiding officer is on leave.
23 Mar 2010	The defendant seeks adjournment on the ground that the main counsel is not available.
03 May 2010	Adjournment sought on behalf of the parties
26 May 2010	The file is not traceable.
9 Jul 2010	An application under Section 151 CPC for treating No. 4 as a preliminary issue. Dismissed with a cost of Rs 2000.
9 Aug 2010	Application for adjournment filed.
27 Sep 2010	The presiding officer is on leave.
23 Oct 2010	For final arguments.
18 Dec 2010	For final arguments.
22 Jan 2011	For final arguments.
05 Feb 2011	For final arguments.
26 Feb 2011	Sought adjournment on the ground that the matter regarding cost is pending in the Hon'ble Supreme Court.

In the same judgment, the apex court talked at length about the reasons behind judicial delay while referring to the seminal work by Senior Advocate Arun Mohan. The judgment reads:

> Dr Arun Mohan, the learned amicus curiae, has written an extremely useful, informative and unusual book titled *Justice Courts and Delays*. This book also deals with the main causes of delay in the administration of justice. He has suggested some effective remedial measures. We would briefly deal with the aspect of delay in the disposal of civil cases and some remedial measures and suggestions to improve the situation. According to our considered view, if these suggestions are implemented in proper perspective, then the present justice delivery system of civil litigation would certainly improve to a great extent.

According to Dr Arun Mohan, 90 per cent of our court time and resources are consumed in attending to uncalled-for litigation, which is created only because our current procedures and practices hold out an incentive for the wrong-doer. Those involved receive less than full justice and there are a greater number than those involved who suffer injustice because they have little access to justice. This includes lack of awareness and confidence in the justice system.

According to Dr Arun Mohan, in our legal system, uncalled-for litigation gets encouragement because our courts do not impose realistic costs. The parties raise unwarranted claims and defences and also adopt obstructionist and delaying tactics because the courts do not impose actual or realistic costs. Ordinarily, the successful party usually remains uncompensated in our courts and that operates as the main motivating factor for unscrupulous litigants. Unless the courts, by appropriate orders or directions, remove the cause for motivation or the incentives, uncalled-for litigation will continue to accrue, and there will be expansion and obstruction of the litigation. Court time and resources will be consumed and justice will be both delayed and denied.

According to Dr Arun Mohan, the lesser the court's attention towards full restitution and realistic costs, which translates as profit for the wrongdoer, the greater would-be the generation of uncalled-for litigation and exercise of skills for achieving delays by impurity in presentation and deployment of obstructive tactics.

According to him, the cost (risk)-benefit ratio is directly dependent on what costs and penalties will the court impose on him; and the benefit will come in as the other 'succumbing' en route and/or leaving a profit for him, or even if it is a fight to the end, the court still leaving a profit with him as unrestituted gains or unassessed short levied costs. Litigation perception of the probability of the other party getting tired and succumbing to the delays and settling with him and the court ultimately awarding what kind of restitution, costs and fines against him—paltry or realistic. This perception ought to be the real risk evaluation.

In *Ramrameshwari Devi and Ors vs Nirmala Devi and Ors,* the Supreme Court suggested some measures to curb delays in civil matters. The court stated,

> The main question which arises for our consideration is whether the prevailing delay in civil litigation can be curbed. In our considered opinion the existing system can be drastically changed or improved if the following steps are taken by the trial courts while dealing with the civil trials.
>
> 1. Pleadings are the foundation of the claims of parties. Civil litigation is largely based on documents. It is the bounden duty and obligation of the trial judge to carefully scrutinise, check, and verify the pleadings and the documents filed by the parties. This must be done immediately after civil suits are filed.
> 2. The court should resort to the discovery and production of documents and interrogatories at the earliest according to the object of the Code. If this exercise is carefully carried out, it would focus on the controversies involved in the case and help the court in arriving at the truth of the matter and doing substantial justice.
> 3. Imposition of actual, realistic or proper costs and or ordering prosecution would go a long way in controlling the tendency of introducing false pleadings and forged and fabricated documents by the litigants. The imposition of heavy costs would also control unnecessary adjournments by the parties. In appropriate cases the courts may consider ordering prosecution otherwise it may not be possible to maintain the purity and sanctity of judicial proceedings.
> 4. The court must adopt a realistic and pragmatic approach in granting mesne profits. The court must carefully keep in view the ground realities while granting mesne profits.
> 5. The courts should be extremely careful and cautious in granting ex-parte ad interim injunctions or stay orders. Ordinarily, short notice should be issued to the defendants

or respondents and only after hearing concerned parties appropriate orders should be passed.

6. Litigants who obtained ex-parte ad interim injunction on the strength of false pleadings and forged documents should be adequately punished. No one should be allowed to abuse the process of the court.
7. The principle of restitution be fully applied pragmatically to do real and substantial justice. Every case emanates from a human or a commercial problem and the court must make serious endeavours to resolve the problem within the framework of law and in accordance with the well-settled principles of law and justice.
8. If in a given case, ex-parte injunction is granted, then the said application for grant of injunction should be disposed of on merits, after hearing both sides as expeditiously as may be possible on a priority basis and undue adjournments should be avoided.
9. At the time of filing of the plaint, the trial court should prepare a complete schedule and fix dates for all the stages of the suit, right from filing of the written statement till pronouncement of judgment and the courts should strictly adhere to the said dates and the said timetable as far as possible. If any interlocutory application is filed then the same be disposed of in between the said dates of hearings fixed in the said suit itself so that the date fixed for the main suit may not be disturbed.
10. According to us, these aforementioned steps may help the courts to drastically improve the existing system of administration of civil litigation in our courts. No doubt, it would take some time for the courts, litigants and advocates to follow the aforesaid steps, but once it is observed across the country, then the prevailing system of adjudication of civil courts is bound to improve.

An important initiative was taken to tackle long-pending cases by setting up of 'Arrears Committees' in high courts and district courts. A resolution was passed for setting up such committees at chief justices' conference held in April 2015. The primary objective of these committees is to clear cases pending for more than five years. To achieve this goal, arrears committee has been constituted under the supervision of district judge and Supreme Court as well. The arrears committee in the Supreme Court is responsible for creating and implementing strategies to reduce the backlog of cases in high courts and district courts. Additionally, an online portal has been developed that allows all high courts to report on their compliance with the guidelines of the Malimath Committee Report's arrears eradication scheme.

One of the main reasons for the significant delay in the justice system is the large number of cases that are waiting to be processed. However, this backlog is just a symptom of a more significant issue that plagues the entire justice delivery system. One of the most pressing issues is the lack of adequate infrastructure, both material and human, which will be discussed in Chapter 3.

This backlog of cases is a serious problem because it delays justice. The law has the potential to be misused, and unfortunately, the police have, in some cases, misused their power to prosecute innocent people. It is the judiciary that has come to the rescue by either averting a wrong or remedying it by punishing the guilty. If justice is not delivered in a timely manner, people will be left to fend for themselves, which would be a significant injustice.

In October 2022, the Supreme Court acquitted a man who was sentenced to death for the alleged murder of his wife and his four kids. While acquitting the accused, the apex court said, 'Without any hesitation and with disappointment, we state that the case on hand is one of most perfunctory investigations.' If it would not have been for the apex court the accused man would have been banished for life for a crime which the apex court found the prosecution could not establish beyond the reasonable doubt.

How far the police can misuse its power if it does not have fear of justice can be gauged from the facts of a case in which the special CBI court in Mohali, Punjab convicted three cops and awarded them life sentences for staging a fake encounter.

In April 1992, a youth named Harjit Singh was picked up by the police from the Thathian bus stand in Sathiala, Amritsar. Thirteen days later he along with two others—Lakhwinder Singh and Jaspinder Singh—all in their twenties, were killed in an encounter. His father filed a writ petition before the Punjab and Haryana High Court, alleging that his son was murdered in a fake encounter.

In December 1992, the high court ordered a judicial inquiry into the case by the District and Sessions Judge, Chandigarh, who submitted a report on the matter in 1995. In 1997, the high court finally transferred the investigation of the case to the CBI, which registered a case in this regard in 1998. Thirty-one years later, on 14 September 2023, three cops were given life imprisonment for killing the three youths in a fake encounter.

The inordinate delay can be gauged from the fact that the 1992 encounter case had nine accused cops, of which three were sentenced and one was a proclaimed offender, while the others died during the trial. Also, the CBI had listed fifty-five witnesses, but due to delay in statements, only twenty-seven witnesses could be recorded as many others had died.

While justice was served, a valid question that may arise is at what cost. Does not more than three decades of wait—which saw the death of many accused and witnesses—render the entire meaning of justice meaningless? Is it not the fact that if a case drags for three decades, it gives the perpetrators of crime a sense of impunity that they can get away even after committing a crime and in the case when they will be held guilty of their crime they must have already spent their entire life freely.

As it is said and often stressed upon, justice should be manifestly seen to be done, as the purpose of criminal justice is not to punish but also to send a message that a wrong will be remedied and wrongdoers will be held accountable.

Delay in dispensing justice erodes the faith in it. And, nothing can be more detrimental to the functioning of a society than the erosion of the faith of its people in the justice delivery system.

'First the alien, then the Jew ... I did no more than you let me do,' reads the line of the poem *The Hangman* by Maurice Ogden. We are the bystanders in the murder of justice sans the realisation we can be the roadkill one day if the wheels of justice keep on moving in the same fashion.

We do not realise the fact that delayed justice is a violation of the fundamental rights and values of democracy. More than that delayed justice violates the trust people have put in the system. It is a betrayal of the promise of justice for all. It is the source of frustration, despair, and legitimacy crisis.

The author spoke to various lawyers who shared their experiences regarding the judicial delay. One of them, Avijit Saxena, who practises at Allahabad High Court shared his experience, which was eye-opening and is reproduced here verbatim for the benefit of the readers:

> In Allahabad High Court the system is highly stressed because of the sheer number of cases pending before it and the humongous filings happening every day. This results in the literal breaking down of the filing system, and the listing system and in turn causes huge delays. The high court has introduced a new digital case monitoring system but that has yet to show its effects fully.
>
> A case once heard at the fresh stage, if remaining pending, goes into the general list of cases pending. There it gets lost amidst the

sheer volume of cases pending and then getting it listed again for hearing is a major problem. The lawyers keep on filing listing applications to get the case listed again but it never works out.

This in turn results in huge delays while the case remains pending, and the client is the ultimate sufferer.

I have had cases going as far back as 1979 which are still pending. In one of the cases (W.P. no. 6727/1979 – Ranjit Singh vs DDC) relating to consolidation proceedings undertaken in the year 1978, the case is still pending adjudication with the main petitioner dead, his son also dead during the litigation and now his grandson is fighting the case on his behalf. The acuteness of the problem can be ascertained by the fact that a substitution application (requesting the court to substitute a dead party with his legal heir) filed in the same case in the year 2002 is still pending for disposal! Now without substituting a dead party with his legal heir, a case cannot proceed further. So when the substitution application is itself pending for the last 16 years, how can anyone expect the main matter to be disposed of in the near future? In such cases which have been pending since the 1980s, 90s, the clients themselves give up any hope of resolution and instead move on with their lives. They stop communicating with the advocates and when such cases are finally listed for hearing, the advocate concerned doesn't have any idea what his client actually wants. This results in the cases not being contested and being dismissed in default or being disposed of as being too old.

Having entered the litigation scene of Allahabad in 2016, I sometimes find cases being listed which were filed by my father when he was a practising advocate in the 1980s before being elevated as a high court judge and subsequently retiring as well.

His name still comes up as the attorney of record in such cases and then I have to inform the court of the changed circumstances.

One such case was where a man met with an accident due to the reckless driving of a minivan in 1989. His entire left hand and leg were shattered, and he had to endure long and expensive treatment, and he lost his job as well. When he brought a claim against the owner of the minivan the Motor Accidents Claim Tribunal awarded just Rs 3000 to him despite recording a clear finding of negligence on the part of the minivan's driver.

My father filed an enhancement appeal before the high court. The court issued notice in 1989 itself but since then the matter remained pending and never came up for hearing again. Finally, it was listed for a final hearing in September 2018 where it was dismissed as having become infructuous for being too old. In this case, the client never showed up in 2018 to inform his lawyers about what is his condition now.

There are similar cases in which retired persons approach high court to get their retiral benefits like pension and gratuity which have been stopped by various bureaucrats and clerks on one pretext or another. Such matters remain pending while the court seeks a response from the concerned government departments. The govt. departments are notorious for not filing their counter affidavits against any petition in time and usually, it takes them 2-3 years and stern warnings of the court to finally give a truncated reply. Then the final adjudication takes another year or two making the said retired person wait even longer to get what was legally and rightfully his from the very beginning. One such case of mine pending before the high court is W.p. 66441/2013 – Chandrapal Yadav vs the State of U.P. wherein the client is still waiting for his lawful retiral dues for the last 5 years and counting. There are numerous cases where the clients are still waiting for their matters to be listed, heard and adjudicated finally.

It must also be seen as to how we treat our litigants. The very people because of which this large high court works, i.e., clients and the common public have very little or no facilities for them in the high court. Imagine a poor old lady travelling from a distant village to the high court in the peak summer months of April-May - she won't get a seat to sit on and wait for her case, there are no toilets for women clients (or for that matter even male clients ... a few stinky, dirty toilets are scattered around which are shared by male lawyers and litigants), no proper drinking water facilities, etc. We must introspect on these things as to whether our clients deserve such treatment when it is their hard-earned money which keeps the entire system functioning.

CHAPTER 2

Heavy Cost of Justice

Until the first week of February 2016, Kanhaiya Kumar was living a comparatively nondescript student life as the president of the Jawaharlal Nehru University Student Union (JNUSU). His fame was confined to the large expanse of the JNU campus. However, in the second week of February, he suddenly became part of the public imagination following his arrest in an alleged sedition case.

His arrest created a wave of protests, and he became an overnight sensation. Kumar hailed from Begusarai in Bihar. His father was paralyzed, and his mother worked as an Anganwadi worker, earning only Rs 3000 per month. The most obvious concern for Kumar and his family would have been the legal aid required to secure his bail and later during the trial. But riding on his newfound fame, Kumar could get India's most prominent legal stalwarts to defend him.

Former Attorney General of India and eminent lawyer Soli Sorabjee led a battery of senior advocates that included Indira Jaising, Vrinda Grover, and Raju Ramachandran to defend Kumar.

Given his modest background, Kumar's chances of affording even one of them for a single appearance were as dim as his chances of being convicted in the sedition case he was charged. But Kumar was a 'rockstar activist', and the legal eagles decided to defend him pro bono. But not everyone is as lucky as Kumar, not even a senior ranking bureaucrat or, by his own admission, a Supreme Court judge.

Accused in a coal block allocation scam, former union coal secretary H.C. Gupta moved a special court in August 2016, seeking to surrender his bail, saying he wanted to 'face trial from inside jail'. The reason was that he could not bear the financial burden of litigation. His decision raised an important question. Has justice become so expensive in India that it has become evasive even for a senior-ranking bureaucrat?

The question may find an answer in the honest confession of a senior advocate and politician, Manish Tewari. He was the union minister of information and broadcasting in the Congress government. While speaking at an event in 2013, Manish Tewari informed the audience that the high cost of litigation was not only keeping the poor from getting justice but even making it unfordable for the upper middle class.[1]

As reported by *The Business Standard*, he said, 'We are in a very strange conundrum whereby the cost of litigation in this country has become increasingly high and it is not only excluding the poor or the disempowered or the marginalised, it is excluding very large swathes of the upper middle class or the salaried people.'[2]

What he said further might throw light on the dire state of the justice delivery system when it comes to access to justice. Tewari said, 'I often joke to myself that the salary I draw as a minister, God forbid that if I have to go to court or something, I may not be able to afford Mr Sidhu's daily fees.' (He was referring to his senior lawyer friend Anmol Rattan Sidhu who was present at the event.) Pointing that the high cost of litigation is a 'great challenge' before the judiciary system, he said, 'If a person who feels that he is aggrieved and believes he has a chance to have his day in court does not decide to exercise that option merely because he is not able to afford it, I think that is an extremely sad day not only for democracy but also for legal the profession collectively.'[3]

Echoing Tewari's voice, the former Supreme Court judge B.S. Chauhan said in 2017 that the Indian legal system is 'so complicated' and expensive that poor people are denied access and that even he would not be able to afford 'big lawyers'.[4]

It should not come as a surprise because what Justice Chauhan said in 2017 was highlighted by the Law Commission of India in 1988 in its 128th report. The report reads, 'Of the many numerous ills with which judicial system as in vogue in the country is suffering, the one which has attracted the attention of all those concerned with the court and interested in its functioning is the high cost of litigation in Indian courts.'

The Law Commission stated that it was informed that top members of the legal fraternity in the Supreme Court charge more often at the rate of Rs 1 lakh. One can safely assume that the fee for top lawyers in the Supreme Court is between Rs 5 and Rs 15 lakh per hearing. On the other hand, even in the high court it is between Rs 50,000 and Rs 2 lakh for top senior lawyers.

T.S.R. Subramanian, former cabinet secretary and one of the finest bureaucrats India has produced, had told the author in 2016, 'The expenses in the higher courts are astronomical. The lawyers have made it a practice to earn adjournments somehow. As they charge a hefty amount per appearance, the adjournments suit them. This is a racket that needs to be stopped from functioning.'

The inadequacies of the legal aid system in India push millions of litigants–the majority of whom belong to the economically weaker section (a fact highlighted in various reports)–to hire 'expensive' courtroom heroes, making justice impossible for many.

On several occasions, the apex court has highlighted unequal access to justice through its judgments. Still, hardly any serious attempt has been made to ensure 'justice for all'.

While dismissing the anticipatory bail plea of IPS officer P.P. Pandey, accused in the Ishrat Jahan fake encounter case, Justice B.S. Chauhan and Justice S.A. Bobde (who later became chief justice of India) in August 2013 observed, 'We are sorry to say that the court's time is being used by senior advocates and big criminals. We can say on oath that only 5 per cent of the time is being used for common citizens, whose appeals are waiting for twenty or thirty years. This court has become a safe haven for big criminals. You come here for the sixth or eighth time for anticipatory bail and we should hear as if we were a trial court.'

In yet another case involving former Haryana chief minister Om Prakash Chautala, who was serving a ten-year jail term in a corruption case and had sought an extension of his interim bail, a bench of Justice H.L. Dattu (who later became chief justice of India) and Justice S.J. Mukhopadhyay observed, 'Sometimes, I wonder at my system. Here is an appeal of the year 2013 which gets a quick hearing. In how many cases are we doing so? That is why poor man feels that the system cares only for known persons and the unknown persons (common man) gets ignored.'

In 1850, the Supreme Court of the United States in *Stockton vs Ford* had observed, 'There are few of the business relations of life involving a higher trust and confidence than that of attorney and client, or, generally speaking, one more honourably and faithfully discharged; few more anxiously guarded by the law, or governed by sterner principles of morality and justice; and it is the duty of the court to administer them in a corresponding spirit, and to be watchful and industrious, to see that confidence thus reposed shall not be used to the detriment or prejudice of the rights of the party bestowing it.'

Ironically, all benchmarks stated in the judgment seem to be eroding.

The bewilderment of the 'My Lords' at the unequal access to justice was obvious. But the irony rests elsewhere. The majority of lawyers who are elevated to judgeship know the rules of the game. Then why do they allow justice to evade the poor? Through its various landmark judgments, the apex court has addressed concerns that perhaps touch every aspect of its citizen's life. From environmental concerns to administration, all have been regulated by the higher judiciary time and again. Then, what stops them from regulating the ground that underpins the entire judicial process?

In this respect, Kaleeswaram Raj, a lawyer practising in the Supreme Court of India and the High Court of Kerala, made an important observation in his article in *The Hindu* in March 2014. He said,

> In a Maharashtra case, *M.P. Vashi vs Union of India*, the levy of exorbitant fees by senior lawyers was the matter in issue. Vashi argued that most of the designated lawyers, by making use of their star value and face value, charge unfair fees. He submitted that a kind of monopoly is being created in the business, detrimental to the interest of the common man at 'the other side' who is unable to afford such highly priced lawyers. Unfortunately, the Bombay High Court was not inclined to accept the contention and a historical opportunity for institutional introspection was lost.

While the fact remains that Rs 5 to 10 lakh per hearing charges can be peanuts for corporate houses embroiled in legal battles, or a 'superstar' making Rs 200 crore a film, or even for a 'superstar activist', it is the ordinary people who constitute a major part of the litigants and have to give up all hopes of justice as it is very expensive.

According to the Access to Justice Survey 2015–16, conducted by Bengaluru-based think tank DAKSH, 90 per cent of the litigants earn less than Rs 3 lakh per annum and the median expected cost of litigation for this group is approximately Rs 16,000.[5]

The high cost of litigation and resulting unequal access to justice is an issue that has been highlighted on several platforms. In 2017, the then president of India Ramnath Kovind, while inaugurating the National Law Day Conference, dwelt on the issue. He remarked, 'India has acquired a reputation of an expensive legal system. In part, this is because of delays but there is also a question of affordability of fees. The idea is that a relatively poor person cannot reach the doors of justice for a fair hearing only because of financial or similar constraints while it is in our constitutional values and republic ethics. It is a burden on our collective conscience.'[6]

Indeed, the burden on the collective conscience looks too heavy when we do some data crunching. As per the Access to Justice Survey 2015–16, civil litigants spend 497 per day on average for court hearings. They incur a loss of Rs 844 per day due to loss of pay. Criminal litigants spend Rs 542 per day for court hearings on average and incur a cost of Rs 902 per day due to loss of pay. When this is put in the context of their earnings, which according to the same survey (for 90 per cent of them) is less than Rs 3 lakh, both the amounts—one spent on court hearing and the resulting loss of pay—assume colossal significance.

The Law Commission in its 128 Report stated, 'Economic disability of any kind shall not preclude a man from having access to justice. Whatever strata of the society he comes from the affluent or the impoverished, each should have access to justice unimpeded by any kind of economic barrier.'

The economic barrier does play a significant impediment to access to justice. According to the *Access of Justice Report 2015-16,* the main reason individuals are unable to meet the conditions for bail is due to a lack of sufficient funds. In the survey, 31.3 per cent of the respondents said they had 'no or insufficient money to pay the bail'.[7]

The litigants have to incur several expenses during the course of litigation; this includes advocates' fees, court fees, process fees, travelling expenses of litigants and witnesses, costs for obtaining copies of documents, typing and other miscellaneous expenses, and costs on account of adjournments. While all the components contribute to the litigation cost, the lawyer fee is the most significant part. This is because it comprises the biggest chunk of the total expenditure. In its report on the cost of litigation, the Law Commission gave advocates' fees top place as a component of the cost of litigation. The report acknowledged that the members of the top echelons of the legal profession charge fees for their services, which are not available on a comparative basis in any other profession.

A litigant embroiled in a civil dispute has to fight the case for years, sometimes even for decades, starting from the district court to the Supreme Court. Roughly, they would spend Rs 2-5 lakh. In a criminal case, where the bail petition is the first step, the money spent to seek bail in a district court can vary from Rs 2500-5000. This may also extend to Rs 1 lakh if the bail is difficult to get. In the high court, the amount that one needs to pay to get bail may be as high as Rs 5 lakh.

A lawyer with twenty years of experience at Allahabad High Court informed that in a double murder case, an accused spent two years in jail to get bail and paid approximately Rs 4.5 lakh.

In July 2017, after a fallout with Delhi Chief Minister Arvind Kejriwal, veteran lawyer Ram Jethmalani slapped Kejriwal with a bill amounting to Rs 3.42 crore for representing the former in a defamation case. According to the *Times Now* report, Jethmalani's bill, which was raised on 1 December 2016, quoted Rs 1 crore retainership for representing Kejriwal and an additional Rs 22 lakh per appearance. Jethmalani had made eleven appearances till then, which led to a total of Rs 3.42 crore, even before the cross-examination stage was over.[8]

When it comes to the Supreme Court and its senior counsel, the amount spent seeking their service is astronomical. According to a report published by *The Mint* in September 2015, based on an interview done by *Legally India*, 'Most of the "class 1" seniors (although there is no actual such term for them) can be retained to represent clients on ordinary matters in the Supreme Court for between Rs 5 lakh and Rs 7 lakh'.[9]

Here are the fees charged by senior lawyers in the Delhi High Court and the Supreme Court.[10]

Approximate Delhi Senior Counsel Rates/Per Appearance	Supreme Court Range (in lakh)	Delhi High Court Range (in lakh)
Late Ram Jethmalani	More than 25	More than 25
Fali Nariman	8–15	
K.K. Venugopal	5–7.5	7–15
Gopal Subramanium	5.5–15	11–16.5
P. Chidambaram	6–7	7–15
Harish Salve	6–15	6–15
A.M. Singhvi	6–11	7–15
C.A. Sundaram	5.5–16.5	
Dushyant Dave	5.5–10	5.5–10
Salman Khurshid	More than 5	8–11
Parag Tripathi	5–7	5–10
K.T.S. Tulsi	5–6	8–9
Kapil Sibal	5–15	9–16
Late Shanti Bhushan	4.5–6	4.5–6

Ranjit Kumar	4–5	
L. Nageswara Rao	3–5	
Siddharth Luthra	3.5	4–5
Rajeev Dhavan	3–5	
Balbir Singh	2.7	1.7
Gopal Jain	2.2–3	2.2–3
Ajit Sinha (Former Judge)	2–5	
Raju Ramachandran	2–4	
Shyam Diwan	2–4	
K.V. Vishwanathan	2–3	
Dhruv Mehta	2–25	2.75
Harin Raval	1.65–3.3	2.2–3.5
Indu Malhotra	1–3	
Jayant Bhushan	1–2.2	
Ravi Sikri	0.75–1 or more	

The following is a list of fees charged by senior lawyers practising in the Delhi High Court.[11]

Delhi High Court Lawyer	Amount Charged (in lakh)
A.S. Chandhiok	5–7
Rajiv Nayar	4–5.5
Arvind Nigam	3–3.5
Sandip Sindhwani	3
Sandip Sethi	2.5–3.3
Pinky Anand	2–3
Pratibha Singh	1.5–2
Joy Basu	1.5
Meet Malhotra	1.5
Sudhir Nandrajog	1.1
Amit Sibal	1–3.5
Dayan Krishnan	0.55–1.1
Geeta Luthra	0.5–1

As can be deduced from the given tables, lawyers' fees in India are largely unregulated. Certain rules do exist, but they are non-binding. The Supreme Court Rules 2013 permit a lawyer to charge a maximum of Rs 8000 per hearing. It also states different fees for different sets of litigation work.

The fee payable to advocates has been tabulated below.[12]

1	Defended appeals, suits, or references under Article 143 or Article 317(1) of the Constitution or under any statute or defended petitions under Article 32 of the Constitution.	Leading counsel	24,000	24,000
		Associate advocate, if any advocate-on-record for instructing	12,000	6,000
2	Undefended appeals.	One fee	14,000	No refresher
3	Petitions for special leave (or appeals on a certificate heard ex-parte).	Leading counsel	8,000	No refresher

		Advocate-on-record when not pleading but only instructing	4,000	No refresher
4	Undefended petitions under Article 32 of the Constitution.	Leading counsel	15,000	7,500
		Advocate-on-record when not pleading but only instructing	8,000	4,000
5	Notices of motion other than petitions under Article 32 of the Constitution when opposed.	Leading counsel	15,000 per appearance	No refresher
		Advocate-on-record	8,000 per appearance	No refresher
6	Petitions in courts for review.	Leading counsel	15,000	No refresher
		Advocate-on-record	10,000	No refresher
7	Opposed applications for investigations in chambers.	One fee	10,000	

8	Unopposed motions and chamber applications and review applications in taxation.	One fee	5,000	
9	Attending taxation or hearing judgment.	One fee	2,500	
10	Attending settlement of index and for taking other steps for preparation of the record.	One fee	5,000	
11	Fee to the amicus curiae appointed by the court.		6,000 up to admission stage and 10,000 on final disposal stage or hearing on regular side after admission/ grant of leave or as directed by the court/chief justice.	

12	Fee to the panel advocate appointed by the registry.		6,000 up to admission stage and 10,000 on final disposal stage or hearing on regular side after admission/ grant of leave, or as directed by the court/chief justice.	

S. No.		Not exceeding (in Rs)
1	To junior advocate for drafting petitions for special leave and petitions under Article 32 of the Constitution inclusive of the affidavits in support of the petition.	12,000
	To the senior for settling petitions for special leave and petitions under Article 32 of the Constitution inclusive of the affidavits in support of the petition.	10,000
2	To junior advocate for drafting other petitions or affidavits (other than formal petitions like petitions for excusing delay and affidavits in them and affidavits of service) or written briefs.	5,500

S. No.		Not exceeding (in Rs)
	To senior advocate for settling other petitions or affidavits (other than formal petitions like excusing delay and affidavits in them and affidavits of service).	7,500
3	To junior advocates for drawing statement of case in appeals, pleadings in suit or special case.	12,000
	To senior advocate for settling statement of case in appeals, pleadings in suit or special case in consultation with junior, if allowed.	18,000
4	Acting fees	
	In appeals (defended and undefended) including suits and references under Article 143 or Article 317(1) of the Constitution or under any statute or defended petitions under Article 32 of the Constitution.	20,000 but not less than 12,000 as the taxing officer may in his discretion allow, having regard to the nature and duration of the 'acting' work involved in the case.
	In undefended petitions under Article 32 of the Constitution.	10,000
	Actual postal and telegraph charges where necessary, are to be allowed at the discretion of the taxing officer.	

While rules may exist that cap lawyer's fees, it is rarely abided by. This became evident in February 2021 in an important case decided by the Bombay High Court. On 9 September 2021, Brihanmumbai Municipal Corporation (BMC) demolished the alleged unauthorised construction at film actor Kangana Ranaut's office-cum-residential bungalow in Pali Hill of Bandra West. Ranaut challenged the BMC decision in the Bombay High Court. The Bombay High Court quashed and set aside an order by BMC to demolish Ranaut's property and held that she was entitled to compensation due to malafide action by the BMC.

The two-judge bench comprising Justice S.J. Kathawalla and Justice R.I. Chagla contended that the BMC's demolition drive 'was with malice' and the 'manner in which the demolition was carried out meant that it was a sinister attempt to silence Kangana'. The case was decided in favour of Kangana Ranaut but there was an offshoot of the entire episode. A petition was also filed in the Bombay High Court challenging the appointment and payment of a 'hefty fee' to Senior Advocate Aspi Chinoy for representing the BMC in Ranaut's case. As reported by *Live Law,* Chinoy was paid Rs 82.5 lakh to defend BMC.

The Bombay High Court rejected the plea and made it clear that 'what fee should be charged by senior advocates and advocates on record, cannot be decided by the court'.

There has been a call for regulating lawyer's fees at different points of time. In various important judgments, the apex court has engaged with this issue. In 2017, the Supreme Court held a discussion on regulating lawyer's fees. Expressing concern over the commercialisation of the legal profession with lawyers charging heavy fees, the apex court asked the central government to make a law regarding regulating advocates' fees by prescribing 'floor and ceiling of advocates' fees.[13]

The Times of India reported that the apex court deprecated the practice of lawyers demanding a share in their client's pecuniary benefits awarded by courts and said it was professional misconduct for which action should be taken against erring advocates. 'Undoubtedly, the legal profession is the major component of the justice delivery system and has a significant role to play in upholding the rule of law. (The) Significance of the profession is on account of its role in providing access to justice and assisting citizens in securing their fundamental and other rights. Can justice be secured with legal professionals failing to uphold professional ethics?' the bench asked.[14]

However, this suggestion did not go well with the majority of members of the bar who decried the suggested regulation. Senior advocate and former Supreme Court Bar Association president, Dhushyant Dave reportedly said, 'The suggestion by the court is completely unconstitutional and illegal. Were the judges who were previously advocates not charging astronomical fees? It is sad that they now feel that fees should be capped. We are not a communist nation, where everything can be regulated. Lawyers have a fundamental right to practice. It is not a right order.'[15]

It may be argued that it is the topmost lawyers who charge these astronomical fees and whether everyone needs to engage them. What difference does their presence make to a case? In this case, an important observation has been made in a book titled *Trial: A Data-Driven Account of The Supreme Court of India* authored by Aparna Chandra, Sital Kalantry, and William H.J. Hubbard. The book addresses in great detail the clout that 'senior advocates' have in our judicial system.

In popular culture, senior advocates are depicted as legal czars whose imposing personalities and erudite and passionate arguments enthral everyone including the judges. The book captures this phenomenon of 'senior advocates' and the influence they wield by sound arguments and numbers. The authors cite numerous reasons for the influence, ranging from the personality cult to the huge practising experience that senior advocates have, which in many cases is more than that of sitting judges of the Supreme Court.

The book, though, data corroborates the hearsay and anecdotes about the kind of influence senior advocates have in the courts. It cites a report by the Vidhi Centre for Legal Policy to press upon its hypothesis. The Vidhi Centre collected a sample of 290 cases from 2014 in which the Supreme Court held an initial hearing on special leave petitions (SLPs). It found that the success rate for petitions in which senior advocates appeared was 60 per cent whereas the success rate for petitions without a senior advocate was 34 per cent.

The authors write, 'Supreme Court's approach to SLP seeks to favour the common person for access to the court, but at the same time, the court heavily favours SLPs argued by the most expensive lawyers in the country. The court gives access with one hand and takes it away with the other.[16]

It is a well-known fact that lawyers' fees and litigation costs increase astronomically as the case lingers for long. One of the reasons why cases linger for an extended period of time is because of adjournments. In this respect, the chief justice of India D.Y. Chandrachud expressed his anguish when he asked the lawyers to refrain from making the Supreme Court a '*tareekh pe tareekh* court'.

The chief justice of India, who was presiding over a three-judge bench, said, 'On the one hand matters are listed on expedited basis, on the other hand, they are mentioned (for urgent hearing), then they get listed and then they are adjourned.... I request the members of the Bar not to file adjournment slips unless it is really, really necessary. I don't want this court to become a "*tareekh pe tareekh*" court.... It doesn't send a good image of our court. It's perhaps for the Bar to ... take corrective measures.'[17] Citing statistics and highlighting the problem, he said, 'There are 178 adjournment slips today and in the last two months—September and October—there were a total of 3688 adjournments requests. On the contrary, I find 2361 matters have been mentioned since September 2023, which comprise 15-20 per cent of the freshly adjourned matters. Per day, from September 1 to November 3, on average, 59 matters are mentioned every day and ironically three times the matters mentioned are adjourned by circulating adjournment slips. They are mentioned three times and get adjourned the moment the matter comes up for hearing.'[18]

Article 39A of the Constitution, part of the Directive Principles of the State Policy, says, 'The State shall secure that the operation of the legal system promotes justice, on the basis of equal opportunity, and shall, in particular, provide free legal aid, by suitable legislation or schemes or in any other way, to ensure that opportunities for securing justice are not denied to any citizen by reason of economic or other disabilities.'

The Constitution stipulates a legal system that ensures justice is not denied to any citizen due to economic or other disabilities. However, the reality is that, like any other commodity, justice is also governed by the law of demand and supply. With more than 4.5 crore cases pending and new ones being added every minute, justice is in great demand. Unfortunately, those responsible for it are not matching in terms of supply, leading to an evident disequilibrium in the system.

Considering this disequilibrium, what the Supreme Court said in *Deepa Bhure & Ors vs Jai Kishan* is of great importance. It said,

> The standards of professional conduct and etiquette which are prescribed in the Bar Council of India Rules do not lay down any guidelines for charging of fees by lawyers. The Rules which

perfunctorily deal with fees charged by advocates are the Bar Council of India Rules. Part VI provides for 'Rules Governing Advocates'. Chapter II therein titled 'Standards of Professional Conduct and Etiquette' prescribes in Section II 'Duty to Client', Rules 11 and 20 of the said Section II read as under:

> '11. An advocate is bound to accept any brief in the courts or tribunals or before any other authority in or before which he proposes to practice at a fee consistent with his standing at the Bar and the nature of the case. Special circumstances may justify his refusal to accept a particular brief.
>
> ...
>
> 20. An advocate shall not stipulate for a fee contingent on the results of litigation or agree to share the proceeds thereof.'

The court recognised that there were severe gaps/lacuna in the rules, which could result in litigants being harassed and frustrated. The court also held that guidelines should be established to regulate advocates' professional fees and also provide a forum for litigants to air their grievances. As a result, there is an urgent need to frame some guidelines. The judgment directed the Bar Council of India to consider framing guidelines prescribing the manner of charging professional fees by lawyers. The said guidelines may broadly address the following issues:

1. Manner of determining the fee consistent with the standing in the bar, as prescribed in Rule 11.
2. Manner of determining the fee consistent with the nature of the case, as prescribed in Rule 11.
3. Reasonable fee that can be charged by lawyers, especially from individual litigants and whether some broad parameters should be prescribed.
4. Reduction of the fee agreement in writing in some form.
5. Charging professional fees in kind and whether the same is permissible.

6. Issuance of receipts upon accepting the professional fees and whether the same ought to be mandatory.
7. Insistence of payment of fees in cash beyond the prescribed limits in law.
8. Demanding and accepting security in any form for professional fee and whether the same is permissible.
9. Permitted modes of recovery of outstanding fees from litigants.

The judgment also directed the Bar Council of India to consider creating a resolution mechanism that includes the appointment of an external ombudsman to handle any complaints from litigants regarding professional fees charged or practices adopted. The resolution of such complaints should also have designated timelines.

Justice loses its very essence and meaning when it comes at a cost that can be borne only by a few. Justice has to be accessible to every citizen irrespective of caste, creed, religion, sex, economic status, or any other qualifier to retain its moral value. Justice loses its 'justness' quotient when it is deliverable based on an external factor apart from what the law prescribes.

CHAPTER 3

Misuse of Law, Travesty of Justice

The French philosopher Voltaire famously cautioned that it is 'better to risk saving a guilty man than to condemn an innocent one'. When an innocent is wrongly condemned, it is the greatest miscarriage of justice. The story of Vishnu Tiwari serves as a sad testimony to this injustice. It was not perpetrated by a powerful state or individual but rather by a law that was misused at the slightest provocation.

Vishnu Tiwari was 23 years old in 2000 when he was charged under different sections of the Indian Penal Code (IPC) and Scheduled Casts and Scheduled Tribes (Prevention of Atrocities) Act, 1989, for allegedly raping a woman belonging to Scheduled Caste. Vishnu was convicted by the trial court in 2003 under Section 376 IPC and sentenced to imprisonment for ten years. He was further convicted under relevant sections of the Scheduled Casts and Scheduled Tribes (Prevention of Atrocities) Act, 1989 and sentenced to imprisonment for life.[1]

Vishnu spent twenty years in jail, not only fulfilling his sentence but also waiting for his appeal to be heard by the high court. Unfortunately, the matter was marked as 'defective' for a period of sixteen years and could not be heard.

In January 2021, Vishnu was finally acquitted by the Allahabad High Court, which lamented the twenty years of Vishnu's incarceration. The court stated, 'In view of the facts and evidence on record, we are convinced that the accused had been convicted wrongly, hence, the trial court's judgment and the impugned order has been reversed and the accused is acquitted.'[2]

A Division Bench comprising Justice Dr Kaushal Jayendra Thaker and Justice Gautam Chowdhary expressed displeasure over the case where a defective appeal was not cured for sixteen years. The bench observed, 'Most unfortunate aspect of this litigation is that the appeal was preferred through jail. The matter remained as a defective matter for a period of sixteen years and, therefore, we normally do not mention the defective appeal number, but we have mentioned the same.'

According to a *Times of India* report, Vishnu's nephew Satyendra said, 'Justice has come but very late. My uncle's wrong conviction has shattered our whole family, both financially and socially. I lost my father, uncle, and grandparents, who died due to shock and social stigma. A major portion of our family land had to be sold to contest the case. As far as my uncle Vishnu is concerned, his entire life has been shattered as he had to spend the best time of his life in jail and that too for no fault of his own.'[3]

The high court also raised an important issue. It said that even after fourteen years of Vishnu Tiwari's incarceration, the State of Uttar Pradesh did not even send the matter to the magistrate for re-evaluating the cases for remission as per the mandate of Sections 432 and 433 of CrPC. Sections 433 and 434 of the CrPC enjoins a duty upon the state government and central government to commute the sentences as mentioned in the said section. The bench, in its judgment, expressed displeasure over the conduct of the State. It said,

> We are pained to mention that even after fourteen years of incarceration, the State did not think of exercising its power for commutation of the sentence of life imprisonment of the present accused and it appears that power of Governor provided under Article 161 of the Constitution of India was also not exercised. The object of Section 432 read with Section 433 of the CrPC is to remit the sentence awarded to the accused if it appears that the offence committed by him is not so grave. In our case, we do not see why the accused is not entitled to remission. His case should have been considered but has not been considered. Remission/commutation of sentence under Sections 433 and 434 of the CrPC is in the realm of power vested in the government. The factual scenario in the present case would show that had the government thought of taking up the case of the accused as per the jail manual, it would have been found that the case of the appellant was not so grave that it could not have been considered for remission/commutation.

The court also held that no offence was committed on Vishnu's part that would have attracted the Scheduled Casts and Scheduled Tribes (Prevention of Atrocities) Act, 1989. The court concluded that while perusing the entire evidence, beginning from the first information report (FIR) to the statements of prosecution witnesses, it did not find that the alleged offence was committed because the prosecutrix belonged to a particular community.

Vishnu's case was neither rare nor one of its kind. In November 2022, the Allahabad High Court rapped the Uttar Pradesh state authorities for not considering the case of a rape accused, who was later acquitted by the high court, for remission even though he had spent over nineteen years in jail.

Aftaf alias Nafees convicted by the Special Judge (SC/ST Act) in 2003 made an appeal in the high court. The appeal was listed in 2004. However, as the order sheet showed, the matter was listed only after a few years and the delay came to be condoned in 2008. The order sheet clearly shows that the matter was never listed for hearing between 2008 and 2022. It was only after the listing application was filed that the matter was listed. Aftaf alias Nafees spent nineteen years in jail before he was acquitted of all charges.

Rape laws and laws penalising atrocities against Scheduled Casts and Scheduled Tribes have been misused and have become a matter of grave concern for the justice delivery system. In the landmark case of *Subhash Kashinath Mahajan vs State of Maharashtra*, the Supreme Court highlighted that the anti-atrocities law that protects Scheduled Castes and Scheduled Tribes from casteist slurs and discrimination has become an instrument to 'blackmail' innocent citizens and public servants.

The court, while issuing a slew of directions in dealing with the cases of all alleged atrocities against the Scheduled Castes and Scheduled Tribes community, made certain important observations:

1. There can be no dispute with the proposition that a mere unilateral allegation by any individual belonging to any caste, when such allegation is clearly motivated and false, cannot be treated as enough to deprive a person of his liberty without independent scrutiny. Thus, the exclusion of provision for anticipatory bail cannot possibly, by any reasonable interpretation, be treated as applicable when no case is made out or allegations are patently false or motivated.
2. If this interpretation is not taken, it may be difficult for public servants to discharge their bona fide functions, and, in given cases, they can be blackmailed with the threat of a false case being registered under the Atrocities Act without any protection of the law. This cannot be the scenario in a civilised society. Similarly, even a non-public servant can

be blackmailed to surrender his civil rights. This is not the intention of the law.

3. Such a law cannot stand judicial scrutiny. It will fall foul of guaranteed fundamental rights of fair and reasonable procedure being followed if a person is deprived of life and liberty.

The apex court issued the following directions to prevent the misuse of provisions of the Scheduled Castes and Scheduled Tribes (Prevention of Atrocities) Act, 1989:

1. There is no absolute bar against the grant of anticipatory bail in cases under the Atrocities Act if no prima facie case is made out or where on judicial scrutiny the complaint is found to be prima facie mala fide.
2. In view of acknowledged abuse of the law of arrest in cases under the Atrocities Act, arrest of a public servant can only be after approval of the appointing authority and of a non-public servant after approval by the senior superintendent of police which may be granted in appropriate cases if considered necessary for reasons recorded. Such reasons must be scrutinised by the magistrate for permitting further detention.
3. To avoid false implication of an innocent, a preliminary enquiry may be conducted by the deputy superintendent concerned to determine whether the allegations make out a case under the Atrocities Act and that the allegations are not frivolous or motivated.
4. Any violation of directions (2) and (3) will be actionable by way of disciplinary action as well as contempt.
5. The bench also directed that a government official cannot be prosecuted on a mere allegation of committing an offence under the Act without the sanction of the appointing authority.

The rampant misuse of this law has forced the courts to criticise it on many occasions. The Madras High Court in *Jones vs State* observed, 'The purpose of bringing SC & ST Act is to put down the atrocities committed on the members of the scheduled castes and scheduled tribes. The law-enforcing authorities must bear in mind that it cannot be misused to settle other disputes between the parties, which is alien to the provisions contemplated under the Act. An Act enacted for laudable purpose can also become unreasonable when it is exercised overzealously by the enforcing authorities for extraneous reasons.'[4]

In September 2023, in a case titled *Nayan Prakash Singh @ Narayan Prakash Singh and Others vs State of Jharkhand and Another*, the Jharkhand High Court highlighted the misuse of the Scheduled Castes and Scheduled Tribes (Prevention of Atrocities) Act, 1989 and found the case to be of 'malicious prosecution' and quashed the case. The bench observed, 'The special law of the SC/ST Act has been enacted to protect the interest of the marginalised section of the Society and it is not intended to be used as an instrument of persecution to settle scores.'[5]

In August 2023, the Karnataka High Court acquitted two brothers charged under the Scheduled Castes and Scheduled Tribes (Prevention of Atrocities) Act. The court said that false cases under the act and IPC are clogging the criminal justice system. The judgment reads,

> 'This case would form a classic illustration of misuse of the provisions of the Act and the penal provisions under the IPC. It is such cases that clog the criminal justice system and consume considerable time of the courts, be it the Magistrates Court, Court of Session or this Court, while genuine cases where litigants have actually suffered would be waiting in the pipeline. On the entire gamut of consideration made hereinabove, what would unmistakably emerge is misuse and abuse of the provisions of

the Act. This case forms a classic illustration of scores and scores of cases where the provisions of the Act are misused for ulterior motives or pressurise the accused in collateral proceedings.'[6]

Section 498A of IPC

On 5 May 2022, a businessman from Odisha named Rahul Agarwal committed suicide by jumping off a building. After the tragic incident, a video surfaced on various social media platforms in which the deceased was seen narrating his ordeal of being 'falsely implicated' in a dowry harassment case (booked under Section 498A of the IPC) by his wife and her family. His parents too were accused in the case and the deceased expressed his helplessness at not being able to do anything in that regard. Hopelessness pushed him to end his life.

The principle of presumption of innocence till proven guilty shifts the burden of proving the guilt to the prosecution. But in some instances like those related to Section 498A of the IPC, the burden is shifted to the defendant, who is left at the mercy of the prosecution including the police, till he proves his innocence.

Presumption of innocence till proven guilty is a fundamental postulate of criminal justice that is sometimes deliberately weakened to ensure 'sure-shot justice' to underprivileged or hitherto disadvantaged classes. However, the entire purpose of such law fails or rather backfires when it is used as 'weapons rather than as shields' by those for whom it was created to act as a safeguard.

Section 498A of the IPC is one such law that is now often used as a weapon to settle personal scores rather than being used as a shield against the harasser. In 1983, Section 498A was introduced in the IPC, which states that whoever, being the husband or the relative of the husband of a woman, subjects such woman to cruelty shall be punished with imprisonment for a term that may extend to three years and shall also be liable to fine.

The reason for introducing this section was highlighted in the statement of objects and reasons of the Act. It stated, 'The increasing number of dowry deaths is a matter of serious concern. Cases of cruelty by the husband and relatives of the husband, which culminates in suicide by or murder of helpless women concerned constitute only a small fraction of the cases involving such cruelty. It is, therefore, proposed to amend the Indian Penal Code, the Code of Criminal Procedure, and the Indian Evidence Act suitably to deal effectively not only with cases of dowry death but also cases of cruelty to married women by their in-laws.'

The law, which was enacted to provide a shield to a married woman from harassment by her husband and his family, has been misused to a great extent, a fact that has been acknowledged by the Supreme Court in its various judgments. In 2014, the Supreme Court made some important observations in relation to the abject misuse of Section 498A. In its judgment titled *Arnesh Kumar vs the State of Bihar*, the apex court held that the law was enacted to combat the menace of harassment to a woman at the hands of her husband and his relatives, but the 'fact that Section 498A is a cognisable and non-bailable offence has lent it a dubious place of pride amongst the provisions that are used as weapons rather than shield by disgruntled wives'.

The judgment reads, 'The simplest way to harass is to get the husband and his relatives arrested under this provision. In quite a number of cases, the bed-ridden grandfathers and grandmothers of the husbands, their sisters living abroad for decades are arrested.'

The apex court, while citing statistics published by the National Crime Records Bureau (NCRB), highlighted certain facts that were worrisome. According to the NCRB data, nearly a quarter of those arrested under this provision in 2012 were women, which evidently means that mothers and sisters of the husbands were 'liberally included in their arrest net'. Another disturbing fact was that while the rate of charge-sheeting in cases under Section 498A of IPC was as high as 93 per cent, the conviction rate was only around 15 per cent, which is the lowest across all heads. The data makes it clear that while the cases were filed easily on the most frivolous grounds and instigations, they fell flat in the court of law as they were not able to withstand the legal scrutiny.

As the crime under Section 498A of IPC is a cognisable offence, it gives immense power to the police to arrest the accused without any judicial approval. While in most cases, the accused is acquitted, the tribulations of trial, litigation cost, and the stigma attached to being an undertrial and accused of a crime together cause irredeemable damage to the life prospects of the accused persons.

Acknowledging this aspect in the same judgment, the apex court noted:

> The arrest brings humiliation, curtails freedom and casts scars forever. Lawmakers know it, and so also the police. There is a battle between the lawmakers and the police and it seems that police have not learnt its lesson; the lesson implicit and embodied in the Criminal Procedure Code (CrPC). It has not come out of its colonial image despite six decades of Independence, it is largely considered as a tool of harassment, and oppression and surely not considered a friend of the public. The need for caution in exercising the drastic power of arrest has been emphasised time and again by courts but has not yielded the desired results. Power to arrest greatly contributes to its arrogance, so also the failure of the Magistracy to check it.

It added, 'Not only this; the power of arrest is one of the lucrative sources of police corruption. The attitude to arrest first and then proceed with the rest is despicable. It has become a handy tool to police officers who lack sensitivity or act with an oblique motive.'

In his video, Rahul Agarwal talked about the same lack of sensitivity by the police who refused to hear his side of the story.

In yet another landmark judgment titled *Preeti Gupta vs the State of Jharkhand*, the apex court dwelt deeply into the issue of rampant misuse of Section 498A. The observations were so strong that they became a reference point for the Law Commission's '243' report, probing the extent of the misuse of the law and suggesting measures to tackle it. In its judgment, the apex court called for a 'serious relook of the entire provision by the legislation'.

The court acknowledged the 'tendency of over implication in a very large number of cases' and made two important observations that are worth noting verbatim here:

(1) The ultimate object of justice is to find out the truth and punish the guilty and protect the innocent. To find out the truth is a Herculean task in the majority of these complaints. The tendency of implicating the husband and all his immediate relations is also not uncommon. At times, even after the conclusion of a criminal trial, it is difficult to ascertain the real truth. The courts have to be extremely careful and cautious in dealing with these complaints and must take pragmatic realities into consideration while dealing with matrimonial cases. The allegations of harassment of the husband's close relations who had been living in different cities and never visited or rarely visited the place where the complainant resided would have an entirely different nature. The allegations of the complaint are required to be scrutinised with great care and circumspection. Experience reveals that long and protracted criminal trials lead to rancour, acrimony, and bitterness in the relationship amongst the parties. It is also a matter of common knowledge that in the cases filed by the complainant if the husband or the husband's relations had to remain in jail even for a few days, it would ruin the chances

of amicable settlement altogether. The process of suffering is extremely long and painful.

(2) The criminal trials lead to immense suffering for all concerned. Even ultimate acquittal in the trial may also not be able to wipe out the deep scars of suffering of ignominy. Unfortunately, a large number of these complaints have not only flooded the courts but also led to enormous social unrest affecting peace, harmony, and happiness of the society. It is imperative for the legislature to take into consideration the informed public opinion and the pragmatic realities in consideration and make necessary changes in the relevant provisions of law.

In a case titled *Kahkashan Kausar alias Sonam vs State of Bihar*, which was decided in February 2022, the apex court held,

> In recent times, matrimonial litigation in the country has also increased significantly and there is a greater disaffection and friction surrounding the institution of marriage, now, more than ever. This has resulted in an increased tendency to employ provisions such as 498A of IPC as instruments to settle personal scores against the husband and his relatives. There is an increased tendency of implicating relatives of the husband in matrimonial disputes, without analysing the long-term ramifications of a trial on the complainant as well as the accused. It is further manifest from the said judgments that false implication by way of general omnibus allegations made in the course of matrimonial dispute if left unchecked would result in misuse of the process of law.

The Malimath Committee on the reforms of the criminal justice system, which submitted its report in 2003, made an important recommendation to check the misuse of the law. The committee recommended making the offence under Section 498A bailable and compoundable.

The Malimath Committee, in its report, observed,

> A less tolerant and impulsive woman may lodge an FIR even on a trivial act. The result is that the husband and his family may be

> immediately arrested and there may be a suspension or loss of job. The offence alleged being non-bailable, innocent persons languish in custody. There may be a claim for maintenance adding fuel to fire, especially if the husband cannot pay. Now the woman may change her mind and get into the mood to forget and forgive. The husband may also realise the mistakes committed and come forward to turn over a new leaf for a loving and cordial relationship. The woman may like to seek reconciliation. But this may not be possible due to the legal obstacles. Even if she wishes to make amends by withdrawing the complaint, she cannot do so as the offence is non-compoundable. The doors for returning to family life stand closed. She is thus left at the mercy of her natal family. This Section, therefore, helps neither the wife nor the husband.

It added,

> The offence being non-bailable and non-compoundable makes an innocent person undergo stigmatization and hardship. Heartless provisions that make the offence non-bailable and non-compoundable operate against reconciliations. It is, therefore, necessary to make this offence (a) bailable and (b) compoundable to give a chance to the spouses to come together.

False Cases under Section 376 of IPC

On 14 November 1991, a woman in the Badaun district of Uttar Pradesh filed a police complaint alleging rape. According to the complainant, her husband had purchased two bighas of land from a man named Shamim. But later, he wanted to sell it for personal reasons. Shamim desired to get back the land sold by him for the same amount, but her husband was reluctant to sell it to him. According to the complainant, Shamim expressed his anger and threatened dire consequences.[7]

About a week before the incident, her husband went to Dehradun for work. Then, on the intervening night of 12/13 November 1991 at around midnight, accused Shamim, along with

Shafiq, Khurshid, and Ashfaq of her village, entered her house. The accused dragged her towards the sugar-cane field and raped her.

The accused were convicted of Section 376 IPC for imprisonment of life. Following this, they appealed to the high court. The high court analysed the property dispute amongst the parties as a strong reason for false implication. The court, in its judgment, stated that it has been found that already a suit was instituted by the wife of accused Shamim for the cancellation of the Salem deed and, therefore, there was no occasion for the accused to unnecessarily insult the prosecutrix by committing rape. According to the doctor, no external injuries were found on her body. As per the internal examination, the vaginal smear did not contain any sperm.

The court held that the prosecution had failed to prove its case beyond reasonable doubt and acquitted the accused of the rape charges and held, 'It is a clear case of false implication due to political rivalry and property dispute.' While the accused were finally acquitted, the false rape case took a heavy toll on their lives. From social banishment to stigmatisation, the accused had to bear it all apart from wasting prime years of their lives to a false and motivated case.

In October 2023, the Supreme Court acquitted a man implicated falsely in a rape case after twenty-three years of ordeal.[8] The incident took place in October 2000. Pappu had requested the complainant, his father-in-law, to send his younger daughter, the prosecutrix in the case to his house to take care of her sister, who had just given birth to a child. The prosecutrix was sent by her father to live for some time at her sister's matrimonial house. More than a month later, the prosecutrix returned to her house and told her mother that while she was in the house of her sister, Manak Chand alias Mani, the younger brother of Pappu, had raped her and thereafter repeated the same offence two to three times.

Initially, considering the relations between the families, an attempt was made to 'settle' the matter and the two families had even agreed to the marriage of the prosecutrix with the accused Manak Chand. But the appellant's family later turned down the offer, which led to the lodging of an FIR.

The accused at the time of the offence was less than 20 years old. The court held that FIR was lodged only after the accused turned down the marriage proposal, a fact pointing out that what was alleged as rape was not rape but could be a consensual act. According to the court, the only factor that could have potentially changed this consensual aspect into a case of 'rape' was the age of the prosecutrix. The medical evidence, however, pointed out that she was older than 16.

The court, most importantly, concluded its judgment with these points:

> First, under these facts, and on the weight of the evidence placed before the Trial Court, we are of the considered opinion that as regarding the age of the prosecutrix, no definite conclusion could have been made. The prosecution could not successfully prove that the prosecutrix was less than 16 years of age at the time of the alleged commission of the crime, and therefore the benefit ought to have been given to the appellant.
>
> Second, as to the factum of rape itself, we are not convinced that an offence of rape is made out in this case as it does not meet the ingredients of rape as defined under Section 375 of the IPC, as we do not find any evidence that may suggest that the appellant even though had sexual intercourse with the prosecutrix, it was against her will or without her consent.

While the court acquitted Manak Chand of the charges of rape, the fact remains that his best years were wasted in court proceedings due to the stigma attached to him of being a rape accused.

In 2016, Rajesh Yadav, a 20-year-old man from Amboli, was acquitted in a rape case after the victim and her mother admitted that they had filed a false case for return of the money the accused had taken from them. Rajesh had languished in jail for one year.

According to *The Times of India* report, Yadav was arrested on 12 February 2015 after the victim claimed that he had promised marriage and had sexual relations with her. The complaint alleged that Yadav, who was married, had forced her to have an abortion and also forced her to steal Rs 1.7 lakh from home. The high court in July 2015 rejected Yadav's plea for bail. Subsequently, a fresh bail plea was filed, this time with an affidavit by the victim claiming that she had lodged the FIR under pressure from her family. She said that she knew Yadav was married and had a consensual sexual relationship with him.

Justice Sadhna Jadhav of Bombay High Court rapped the mother-daughter duo for falsely implicating the youth: 'It is extremely unfortunate that a person had to remain behind bars for almost one year for being falsely prosecuted for a serious offence like (rape) Section 376 of the Indian Penal Code.'[9]

In October 2023, the Supreme Court bench comprising Justice Sanjay Kishan Kaul, Justice Sudhanshu Dhulia, and Justice C.T. Ravikumar in the case titled *Raju and Others vs State of Madhya Pradesh (2008)* held it cannot be lost sight of that rape causes the greatest distress and humiliation to the victim but at the same time a false allegation of rape can cause equal distress, humiliation, and damage to the accused as well. The accused must also be protected against the possibility of false implication, particularly where a large number of accused are involved.

Misusing any law renders its basic purpose of acting as a deterrent useless and poses a grave challenge to the judiciary. The credibility of a criminal justice system depends upon a principle formulated by English jurist William Blackstone in his seminal work *Commentaries on the Laws of England*. The principle states that ten guilty persons should escape than that one innocent suffer.

However, when the presumption of innocence is replaced with the presumption of guilt, the above-mentioned principle goes for a toss and poses a real challenge to a fair trial, often leading to a miscarriage of justice.

CHAPTER 4

Infrastructure Woes

In 2019, the Bombay High Court directed the Brihanmumbai Municipal Corporation (BMC) to provide space to the Maharashtra government on rent until the construction of the magistrate court building in Dadar was completed. The court had issued this directive since the magistrate court premises were too dilapidated to be repaired and needed to be demolished. The court building was not only in a ramshackle state but also inadequate to accommodate all courtrooms as some of them operated from adjacent rental premises.

This was the condition of the court infrastructure in the country's financial capital. If one travels to the hinterlands of Bihar or Odisha, one will find the court infrastructure in a more troubled state.

In a report dated February 2022, *Amar Ujala* reported that a court building in Gurugram had collapsed and a new building would be ready in two years. The building, which was fifty years old, was in a highly dilapidated state. A major accident could have occurred if the balcony had fallen during the day.[1] Similarly, in July 2020, *Dainik Jagran* reported that a part of the chief judicial magistrate (CJM) court's building collapsed in Aligarh, injuring a lawyer.[2] These are not isolated incidents. Court infrastructure across the country is in a poor state.

In December 2023, a division bench of the Delhi High Court expressed displeasure with the Delhi government for its 'complete lack of cooperation in relation to the development of infrastructure for the district courts in Delhi'. The high court called it 'non-cooperation at its peak'.

The court observed, 'Nothing is happening at your end. No funds are being released. You are undertaking six to seven infrastructure projects, none of them is functioning at the moment. There is a lack of cooperation ... neither staff is being given, nor finances are given. No infrastructural project is being cleared.' The court further noted that in Patiala House Court, one courtroom was shared by three judges and some judges came to the court only to record evidence in cases.[3]

In one of the previous hearings, the bench noted a shortage of space and budget in all district courts in the city. The number of courtrooms available was not commensurate with the sanctioned strength of judicial officers. The court opined that ninety-nine newly recruited officers were undergoing training at the Delhi Judicial Academy, with more expected to join shortly. After completion of their training, it would not be possible for the High Court of Delhi to allot courts to all these officers on account of the non-availability of courtrooms.[4]

Advocate Ardhendumauli Kumar Prasad filed a petition requesting the preparation of a layout for constructing a 'Judicial Vista'. The purpose of this was to provide better and dignified working conditions for judges, members of the Bar, and registry officials. In April 2022, a Supreme Court bench comprising Justice Vineet Saran and Justice J.K. Maheshwari heard the petition. During the hearing, the judges said that overcrowding in courts was preventing judges from moving around. The plea stated, 'The infrastructure that is available at this Hon'ble Court is disproportionate to the growth of the Court in terms of the number of Judges, the Registry, the Bar, and most importantly the volume of cases. The present Supreme Court complex constructed in 1958 and renovated from time to time is highly inadequate for the purposes of the present size and volume of the Court.'[5]

It is not only judicial bodies that are putrefying from the inside. The infrastructure of quasi-judicial bodies is also a cause for concern. A report by *Live Law* in 2022 revealed, 'The infrastructure at National Company Law Tribunal (NCLT) specifically at NCLT New Delhi is in shambles. The courtrooms are cramped and NCLT Bench V, New Delhi is functioning from a room similar to the size of a small chamber. There is no space for the registry to keep files, the library has a sitting capacity of merely ten people.'[6]

In 2016, social activists Naresh Gosavi and Kailash Sharma filed a public interest litigation in the Bombay High Court, alleging that the Maharashtra State Human Rights Commission (MSHRC) had not received funding for purchasing computers and other equipment for the past two years. The petition further stated, 'Lack of timely appointment of members has resulted in a severe impediment to the protection of human rights and dignity across the state and a massive backlog of cases.'[7]

The third pillar of the state, the judiciary, is in dire need of better infrastructure. While the ministerial houses enjoy lavish maintenance costs running into thousands of crores, the courts are struggling with inadequate facilities and resources. What is the reason behind this disparity? Is it the lack of political will or the inefficiency of the state machinery in using the allocated funds? Moreover, why is it important to have better infrastructure for the judiciary?

As James Bryce has rightly said, 'There is no better test of excellence of a government than the efficiency of its judicial system, for nothing more nearly touches the welfare and security of the average citizen than his knowledge that he can rely on the certain and prompt administration of justice.' Efficiency and promptness of the judiciary cannot be ensured when the infrastructure is in a decrepit state.

The adequacy of judicial infrastructure is critical for reducing the pendency and backlog of court cases. When people fail to get justice, it leads to simmering anger beneath the surface. As a result, the outcome is a travesty of justice. Whether it is the cold-blooded murder of Atiq Ahmed while in police custody or the encounter of four men accused of rape and murder of a young veterinarian in Telangana, all were applauded by the ordinary person because they have had enough.

In 2016, the Bombay High Court, while hearing a petition filed by the Sales Tax Tribunal Bar Association, expressed extreme anguish over the poor state of affairs. The high court observed that it is time that the State 'realises if it cannot support its own judiciary by providing infrastructure and staff, it will not be able to obtain early disposal of cases and pending matters. Just as a police station and other government authorities require support and care from the state in this regard, equally, the judiciary must be on the map and we hope that there will be a change in the mindset and our intervention will be minimal thereafter'.[8]

In one of the hearings, the division bench of Justice S.C. Dharmadhikari and Justice B.P. Colabawalla observed that courts 'are not for lawyers and judges, they are for litigants. If the state is not interested in doing anything, the Bar Associations should start boycotting the courts, in that way maybe these issues will get the state's attention'.

The Bombay High Court was right in criticising the State for overlooking the infrastructural needs of the courts as the primary responsibility of developing infrastructure for the district and high courts rests with the state governments.

The Centrally sponsored scheme for judicial infrastructure, which has been in operation since 1993-94, is a key initiative by the central government to support the development of infrastructure facilities for the judiciary. This scheme primarily focuses on constructing court buildings and residential accommodations for judicial officers of the district and subordinate judiciary. The Department of Justice, under the Ministry of Law and Justice, serves as the nodal ministry for this scheme.

The scheme has been extended from 2021-22 to 2025-26 with a budgetary outlay of Rs 9000 crore, including a central share of Rs 5,307 crore. In addition to court halls and residential quarters, the scheme also covers the construction of lawyers' halls, digital computer rooms, and toilet complexes in the district and subordinate courts. The scheme guidelines were revised in August 2021. To monitor the status of the projects under the scheme, three monitoring mechanisms have been established: a high court-level monitoring committee at the state level, a Central-level monitoring committee in the Department of Justice, and the Nyaya Vikas online monitoring system. A web portal and mobile app named 'Nyaya Vikas' were launched in 2018 to monitor construction projects online. The newer version of the mobile app, launched in April 2020, is now more user friendly and runs on both iOS and Android systems. The fund-sharing pattern under the scheme is 60:40 (Centre: State), 90:10 for eight north-eastern and two Himalayan states, and 100 per cent central funding for the union territories.

Till March 2022, Rs 8758.71 crore has been released under the scheme, of which Rs 5314.40 crore (60.68 per cent) has been released since 2014-15. According to the official estimates, the extension of the scheme will help construct 3800 court halls and 4000 residential units (both new and ongoing projects) for judicial officers of district and subordinate courts, 1450 lawyer halls, 1450 toilet complexes, and 3800 digital computer rooms.

The judicial infrastructure is in a bad state by the government's own admission. The press release detailing the union government's decision to extend the scheme for the development of infrastructure facilities notes that 'several courts are still functioning in rented premises with insufficient space and some in a dilapidated condition without basic amenities' and lack of residential accommodation to all the judicial officers also 'adversely affects their working and performance'.[9]

An all-India survey of 6000 trial courts was conducted in 2021 by the chief justice of India's office, which was part of the then chief justice of India N.V. Ramana's proposal to set up a National Judicial Infrastructure Corporation (NJIC) to develop judicial infrastructure in trial courts. According to a report by *The Print*, the survey indicated a substantial gap in infrastructure and availability of basic amenities in the lower judiciary, such as court halls, residential accommodation, and waiting rooms for litigants in trial courts, especially in smaller towns and rural areas. Only 27 per cent of courtrooms in the subordinate judiciary have computers on judges' desks, while there is still 10 per cent of courts that do not have access to proper internet facilities. Around 22 per cent of trial court complexes do not have women's toilet facilities while 16 per cent do not have such a facility for men either. Only 54 per cent of the total complexes have basic medical facilities and only 620 court complexes still operate from rented premises.[10]

The survey highlighted that while the number of judicial officers in trial courts is approximately 24,280, yet only 20,143 court halls are available.

However, in August 2023, *The Times of India* reported, 'An ongoing effort to develop judicial infrastructure has resulted in the availability of 21,365 court halls against 19,876 judges at present in the subordinate judiciary across the country. Over 2800 court halls and 1640 residential units are under construction.'[11]

It was found that only 55 per cent of the surveyed trial courts have a separate room for staff attached to judges and 54 per cent have drinking water facilities. Only 55 per cent of the courts have centralised filing centres, while meditation halls are available in just 31 per cent. The majority of court complexes lack a waiting area for litigants, with only 33 per cent having this facility. The survey also revealed that over 3900 judges in trial courts reside in rented accommodations. Meeting halls for judges are absent in about 83 per cent of the courts and only 51 per cent have library facilities for judicial officers. Furthermore, the survey pointed out that the trial courts are not adhering to the top court's 2017 judgment mandating all public institutions to be disabled friendly. Of the 6000 courts surveyed, 67 per cent lack provisions to facilitate access for people with disabilities.[12]

While under the present Narendra Modi government, there has been a sharp increase in allocating funds under the Centrally Sponsored Scheme for Judicial Infrastructure, the utilisation of these funds by the state has not been very inspiring.[13] When it comes to implementing a Centrally Sponsored Scheme for Judicial Infrastructure, the results have been far from satisfactory.

According to a report titled *Budgeting Better for Courts: An Evaluation of the Rs. 7460 Crores Released Under the Centrally Sponsored Scheme for Judicial Infrastructure*, considerable confusion exists amongst the state governments on the actual working of this sharing formula. 'The Centre releases its share based on the funds available with it and expects the States to contribute the remaining share depending on the sharing pattern prevailing at the time. Contrary to this, most State governments seem to presume that the Centre will allocate its share keeping in mind the requirement projected by the State in the Action Plan,' said the report.[14]

When the states fail to contribute to their share of funds, the money under the scheme is often left unspent and lapses as a result. There have been instances where the states have redirected a portion of the fund for purposes unrelated to judicial matters.

The report traced the problem with the implementation at two levels: at the ministry level and at the state level. According to the report, lack of accountability is one of the major problems that hinders the effective implementation of the scheme. The second problem highlighted by the report is the arbitrary allocation of funds.

The report read, 'At the level of the DoJ, the overwhelming problem with this Scheme was the lack of measures to ensure transparency and accountability. To provide but one example, the DoJ has so far not released authoritative figures which confirm the number of courtrooms and residential units that have been constructed under this Scheme. The lack of availability of such data makes it difficult to assess the performance of the Scheme and it also raises questions about the record-keeping practices of the DoJ. Similarly, funds released under the Scheme appear to have been distributed amongst different States arbitrarily. The rationale explaining the quantum of funds being released every year by the DoJ is missing in the sanctioning orders issued by the DoJ.'[15]

Additionally, the current scheme design lacks periodic technical and financial audits, making monitoring cost and time overruns difficult. The existing format of the utilisation certificate is inadequate for collecting useful information from state governments.

According to an analysis by Nikhil Majithia, an advocate-on-record at the Supreme Court, 'There are essentially two reasons behind the scheme's tardy progress. First, there is no single ownership of the scheme. The lack of one coordinating agency prevents its successful execution. The Centrally Sponsored Scheme, in its current form, visualises separate state- and central-level monitoring committees. Second, in the central committee, there is no representation of the judiciary as an institution. So, the ultimate consumer of the scheme is absent from the entire process.'[16]

There are several issues hindering the effective implementation of the scheme such as lack of coordination between the different departments of the state government responsible for the implementation of the scheme and inefficient planning and execution in terms of acquisition of land, quality of construction, etc. However, the Nyaya Vikas portal, created by the government to ensure accountability and transparency, can monitor the scheme. But the portal is marred by several problems.

The Department of Justice does not keep any information regarding the appointment of surveyors, moderators, and nodal officers at the state level. The fact that the Department of Justice does not have such information indicates that it is not monitoring progress on the portal. The state governments are unlikely to take the necessary steps to fill in the information as they lack any ownership over the portal. Moreover, the portal is not accessible to the judiciary, advocate bar associations, or the general public, thereby impeding transparency efforts.

In January 2023, delivering the Advocate V.C. Rajagopalachariar memorial lecture at Vellore Institute of Technology, former chief justice of India Justice N.V. Ramana said, 'As States faced funds crunch, they were unable to mobilise their contribution of 40 per cent for judicial infrastructure, leaving the central funds unutilised. Many courts do not have washrooms, libraries and chambers.'[17]

The central government sanctioned Rs 981.98 crore in 2019-20 under the Centrally Sponsored Scheme to the states and union territories to develop infrastructure in the courts. But only a combined five states utilised Rs 84.9 crore, rendering the remaining 91.36 per cent of funds unused. In 2020-21, a major part of the sanctioned Rs 594.36 crore remained unused.[18] Reports have also emerged of alleged divergence of funds for other tasks by state governments.

Infrastructure Woes

Indian judiciary is marred by the lack of proper infrastructure both in terms of physical infrastructure and human resources. In 2021, the then chief justice of India, N.V. Ramana, highlighting the issue of bad infrastructure that the judiciary is grappling with, said, 'Courts in India still operate from dilapidated structures, without proper facilities. Such a situation is severely detrimental to the experience of litigants and lawyers. It is an unpleasant work environment for court staff and judges, making it difficult to effectively perform their functions. We neglected and failed to focus on providing good infrastructure for courts in India after the British left.'[19]

In November 2022, chief justice of India D.Y. Chandrachud called for better infrastructure as it forms 'the core of the Indian Judiciary'. He lamented the 'pitiable' state of facilities and highlighted that in many cases women judicial officers did not even have toilets in courts.

The biggest issue the Indian judiciary is grappling with is the backlog of pending cases. One of the main reasons for this is the insufficient number of judges to handle the existing workload and to deal with the new cases that keep coming in. There are currently many vacancies at each tier of the judiciary. The Supreme Court, for instance, had only 31 judges until November 2023, when three new judges were appointed, bringing it back to its full strength of 34 judges. Meanwhile, in the high courts, out of the sanctioned strength of 1114 judges, only 785 judges are working, leaving 329 posts vacant. Of these 329 vacancies, 119 proposals are being processed by the government and the Supreme Court collegium, while the remaining 210 recommendations vacancies are yet to be received from the high court collegiums. Vacancies in high courts arise due to retirements, resignations, elevations, and an increase in the strength of judges.[20]

How far pendency can be reduced depends upon various factors, which include the availability of physical infrastructure and supporting court staff, the complexity of facts involved, the nature of evidence, the cooperation of stakeholders concerning the bar, investigation agencies, witnesses and litigants, and proper application of rules and procedures.

Other factors that lead to delays in case disposal include the lack of prescribed timeframe by respective courts for disposal of various kinds of cases, frequent adjournments, and lack of adequate arrangements to monitor, track, and bunch cases for hearing. This chapter is focused on physical infrastructure and human resources.

Physical Infrastructure

Subordinate Courts of India: A Report on Access to Justice 2016, without mincing any words, said, 'A judge trying cases for days without end, in makeshift rooms cannot be expected to turn out optimal result; equally, shortage of secretarial and support staff tells on the availability of court services, so vital to ensure timeliness.'[21]

An effective judicial process resulting from a good judicial infrastructure is empirically proved. According to the National Mission for Justice Delivery and Legal Reforms, adequacy of judicial infrastructure is a pre-condition for reducing delays and backlogs in cases. The Supreme Court-constituted National Court Management System (NCMS) says that there is a direct connection between physical infrastructure, personnel infrastructure, digital infrastructure, and pendency.

As per information made available by high courts till April 2022, against a sanctioned strength of 24,521 and working strength of 19,341 judges, presently 20,812 court halls (including 578 rented ones) and 18,338 residential units are available in the district and subordinate courts as of 31 March 2022. Moreover, 2767 court halls and 1651 residential units are under construction.

In October 2021, the then chief justice of India N.V. Ramana emphasised the need for good judicial infrastructure and revealed that almost 20 per cent of judicial officers in the country did not have proper courtrooms to sit in. Of the total sanctioned strength of 24,280 judicial officers, only 20,143 court halls are available, including 620 rented premises. Justice Ramana also mentioned that 26 per cent of the court premises had no toilets for women, 16 per cent did not have toilets for men, and only 54 per cent of courts had purified drinking water facilities.[22]

It is worth noting that even in December 2021, the Law Minister informed the Rajya Sabha that 26 per cent of court complexes in India do not have a separate toilet for women. This was in response to a question raised by Rajya Sabha MP S. Niranjan Reddy who asked whether the government is aware that most court complexes, especially at the subordinate level, do not have safe, private places and washrooms available to women lawyers and women litigants.[23]

Human Resources

In February 2023, the then law minister Kiren Rijiju in a written reply to the Rajya Sabha said that India had approximately 21 judges per million people. Similarly, in December 2023, the Law Minister Arjun Ram Meghwal informed the Lok Sabha that India still had 21 judges per million people. The Law Minister said, 'It can be seen that over a period of time, the strength of the judiciary has seen a marked increase with the district judiciary's working strength of 15,115 judicial officers, as against sanctioned strength of 19,518 in the year 2014, increasing to a working strength of 20,026, as against sanctioned strength of 25,423 in the year 2023.'

However, it should be noted that the data used to calculate this ratio was based on the 2011 census, which reported a population of 1210.19 million. In the last decade, the population has increased by at least 20 crore. Therefore, the actual ratio of judges per million population may be even less than the estimate provided by the Law Ministry.

The Law Commission of India published a report in July 1987 titled *Manpower Planning in Judiciary: A Blueprint*, in which it was observed that the number of judicial officers in India was far less as compared to certain other countries. The Commission recommended that the present strength of 10.5 judges per million population be increased to 50 judges per million population in a phased manner. However, even after 36 years, the ratio remains at a dismal level.

In the case of *All India Judges Association and Others vs Union of India 2001*, the Supreme Court of India stated that an independent and efficient judicial system is one of the basic structures of the Constitution. If a sufficient number of judges are not appointed, justice will not be available to the people, thereby undermining the basic structure. It is well known that justice delayed is justice denied. Time and again, the inadequacy in the number of judges has adversely been commented upon. Not only have the Law Commission and the standing committee of Parliament made observations in this regard, but even the head of the judiciary, namely, the chief justice of India, has had more than one occasion to make observations in regard thereto. Under the circumstances, the Supreme Court felt it was its constitutional obligation to ensure that the backlog of cases is decreased and that efforts are made to increase the disposal of cases. Apart from the steps that may be necessary for increasing the efficiency of the judicial officers, the court was of the opinion that the time had come to protect one of the pillars of the Constitution, namely, the judicial system, by directing an increase, in the first instance, in the judge strength from the existing ratio of 10.5 or 13 per 10 lakh people to 50 judges for 10 lakh people.[24]

The lack of proper infrastructure and an inadequate number of judges has resulted in a sense of helplessness, apathy, and frustration among legal professionals and citizens alike. In 2016, the then chief justice of India T.S. Thakur, addressing the inaugural session of the Joint Conference of Chief Ministers and Chief Justices of High Courts, broke down in the presence of PM Narendra Modi. Justice Thakur highlighted, 'Judges strength has been put in cold storage for the past three decades. You cannot blame the judiciary alone for the high number of pending cases. In some petitions, we have to dispose of ourselves in extremely stressful conditions. I request your government to address the issue.' Justice Thakur made an impassioned plea to the government to help upgrade judicial infrastructure and start addressing the glaring problem of shortage of judges. He said the country needed at least 40,000 judges to handle the 'avalanche' of litigation.

Disputing the numbers cited by Justice T.S. Thakur on the required number of judges, the then union law minister D.V. Sadananda Gowda said that the demand was not backed by any scientific or empirical data. Gowda said that the report cited by Justice Thakur to claim that the country needed 40,000 judges was not based on any scientific research and that he would not want to comment on the exact number for want of concrete data.[25]

According to the rule, the strength of judges in the high courts is reviewed every three years. The data received from the high courts for the triennial review of the judge strength of the high courts are analysed under the guidelines fixed for the increase of the strength, which is based on the number of cases filed and disposed of.

According to the *India Justice Report 2022*, as of December 2022, against a sanctioned strength of 1108 judges, the high courts were functioning with only 778 judges. The subordinate courts were found functioning with 19,288 judges against a sanctioned strength of 24,631 judges.

In July 2022, the then chief justice of India N.V. Ramana while highlighting that that the problem of pendency of cases is 'intensifying' due to the lack of a sufficient number of judges, said the government is yet to clear twenty-three names recommended for various high courts. He said that he was hoping for some forward movement in this regard. An issue that has been affecting court systems across the world relates to the fact that decisions within the regular courts take a long time, the then chief justice of India said in his inaugural address at the Conference on 'Arbitrating Indo-UK Commercial Disputes' at Mansion House, London.[26]

As of 8 December 2023, Law Minister Arjun Ram Meghwal informed the Rajya Sabha that out of the sanctioned strength of 1114 judges in the high courts across the country, only 790 judges are working, leaving 324 positions vacant. As of 4 December 2023, the Law Minister informed that 122 proposals received from high court collegiums for appointment of judges are at different stages of processing. Regarding the creation of new jobs, on 20 December 2023, the Law Minister informed the Lok Sabha that 35 new posts of judges have been created in various high courts across the country in the last five years.

National Judicial Infrastructure Authority of India

In 2010, the Andhra Pradesh High Court Judge Justice V.V. Rao shocked everyone by estimating that the Indian judiciary would take 320 years to clear the backlog of 31.28 million cases pending in various courts at that time.[27]

He had his own approach to arriving at this conclusion, and while one may disagree with him, the fact remains that the Indian judiciary is struggling with a significant backlog of cases, and one of the reasons for this is the poor state of judicial infrastructure.

In April 2022, the then chief justice of India, N.V. Ramana, addressing the Joint Conference of Chief Justices and Chief Ministers, highlighted the fact: 'There is a severe gap between the existing infrastructure and the projected justice needs of the people. The environment of some district courts is such, even lady advocates feel apprehensive about entering courtrooms, let alone female clients. Courts, being temples of justice, should be welcoming and carry the requisite dignity and aura.'[28]

In the same conference, Justice N.V. Ramana highlighted a very important fact. According to him, during the last joint conference of chief justices and chief ministers held in 2016, the sanctioned strength of judges was 20,811, which was increased to 24,112 at the rate of 16 per cent in six years. However, in the corresponding period, pendency in district courts has gone up from 2 crore 65 lakh to 4 crore 11 lakh, which is an increase of 54.64 per cent.

While substantial funds are being allocated under the Centrally Sponsored Scheme for Judicial Infrastructure and through other budgetary provisions, the fact is that the lack of an institutional mechanism to foresee the progress is hampering the prospects of infrastructure development in the judiciary.

Keeping this in mind, Justice N.V. Ramana had mooted the idea of establishing the National Judicial Infrastructure Authority of India (NJIAI), which will be tasked with developing judicial infrastructure and monitoring its progress.

On 21 March 2022, the Ministry of Law and Justice released a press note stating that they received a proposal from the chief justice of India to establish the NJIAI. The purpose of the NJIAI was to provide adequate infrastructure for courts. The proposal suggested that there would be a governing body, with the chief justice of India as patron-in-chief. The NJIAI would act as a central body to plan, create, develop, maintain, and manage the functional infrastructure for the Indian court system as well as identical structures under all the high courts.[29]

In February 2022, stressing the need for NJIAI, Justice N.V. Ramana said, 'Judicial infrastructure needs to be improved. Unfortunately, we are not even meeting the basic minimum standards in this area. It has been my endeavour since assuming the office of CJI, to put in place an institutional mechanism to coordinate and oversee the improvement of judicial infrastructure. Mere allocation of funds is not enough ... I have been pursuing the government for setting up statutory authorities—at the Centre and the states.'[30]

However, the idea of establishing NJIAI did not find many takers. In August 2022, the then union minister of law and justice, Kiren Rijiju informed the Lok Sabha that no consensus had been reached on the proposal of chief justice of India N.V. Ramana. The proposal had been sent to various state governments/union territories for their views on the matter, but no consensus was reached. The issue was also discussed in the Conference of Chief Ministers and chief justices held on 30 April 2022, but the proposal was not agreed upon due to lack of consensus.[31]

E-court

The COVID-19 pandemic has highlighted the importance of technology in various fields, such as education, medicine, and the justice system. While technology played an important role in delivering justice during the pandemic, it has also revealed the need for better digital infrastructure. To augment the digital infrastructure, the Indian government has approved the third phase of the e-courts project, with a financial outlay of Rs 7210 crore to be implemented over four years.

The e-courts project was initiated in 2007 to enable the use of information and communication technology in the Indian judiciary. The second phase of the project was expected to conclude in 2023.

The union cabinet has approved the third phase of the e-courts project. In the third phase, a regime of maximum ease of justice will be established by moving towards digital, online, and paperless courts through digitisation of the entire court records, including legacy records, and by bringing in universalization of e-filing/e-payments through saturation of all court complexes with e-sewa kendras. It will put in place intelligent smart systems enabling data-based decision-making for judges and registries while scheduling or prioritising cases. The main objective of the third phase is to create a unified technology platform for the judiciary, which will provide a seamless and paperless interface between the courts, the litigants, and other stakeholders.[32]

As of 31 January 2023, here is a list of courts where virtual hearings are taking place, along with the cases heard.

S. No.	High Court	No. of Hearings in High Courts	No. of Hearings in District Courts	Total Hearings
1	Allahabad	241,390	4,114,257	4,355,647
2	Andhra Pradesh	380,252	1,412,770	1,793,022
3	Bombay	38,305	80,818	119,123
4	Calcutta	139,053	81,940	220,993
5	Chhattisgarh	103,097	43,160	146,257
6	Delhi	317,729	4,502,342	4,820,071
7	Guwahati, Arunachal Pradesh	2,292	8,128	10,420
8	Guwahati, Assam	266,160	333,777	599,937
9	Guwahati, Mizoram	3,963	13,268	17,231
10	Guwahati, Nagaland	930	650	1,580
11	Gujarat	388,929	192,808	581,737
12	Himachal Pradesh	183,904	100,200	284,104
13	Jammu & Kashmir and Ladakh	257,708	458,532	716,240
14	Jharkhand	218,343	641,727	860,070
15	Karnataka	117,0814	123,066	1,293,880

S. No.	High Court	No. of Hearings in High Courts	No. of Hearings in District Courts	Total Hearings
16	Kerala	160,411	541,229	701,640
17	Madhya Pradesh	668,369	782,248	1,450,617
18	Madras	1,424,427	347,900	1,772,327
19	Manipur	38,695	15,288	53,983
20	Meghalaya	2,859	27,554	30,413
21	Odisha	288,674	247,949	536,623
22	Patna	275,754	2,116,523	2,392,277
23	Punjab & Haryana	581,047	1,873,547	2,454,594
24	Rajasthan	229,688	179,006	408,694
25	Sikkim	482	12,227	12,709
26	Telangana	299,031	190,327	489,358
27	Tripura	10,585	12,564	23,149
28	Uttarakhand	74,705	41,430	116,135
Total		7,767,596	18,495,235	26,262,831

The details of operational e-courts in the country are listed here.[33]

S. No.	High Court	State	Court Complexes	Courts
1	Allahabad	Uttar Pradesh	180	2222
2	Andhra Pradesh	Andhra Pradesh	218	617
3	Bombay	Dadra and Nagar Haveli Daman and Diu Goa Maharashtra	1 2 17 471	3 2 39 2157
4	Calcutta	Andaman & Nicobar Islands West Bengal	4 89	14 827

S. No.	High Court	State	Court Complexes	Courts
5	Chhattisgarh	Chhattisgarh	93	434
6	Delhi	Delhi	5	681
7	Guwahati	Arunachal Pradesh Assam Mizoram Nagaland	14 74 8 11	28 408 69 37
8	Gujarat	Gujarat	376	1268
9	Himachal Pradesh	Himachal Pradesh	50	162
10	Union Territory Jammu & Kashmir and Union Territory of Ladakh	Union Territory of Jammu & Kashmir and Union Territory of Ladakh	86	218
11	Jharkhand	Jharkhand	28	447
12	Karnataka	Karnataka	207	1031
13	Kerala	Kerala Lakshadweep	158 1	484 3
14	Madhya Pradesh	Madhya Pradesh	213	1363
15	Madras	Puducherry Tamil Nadu	4 263	24 1124
16	Manipur	Manipur	17	38
17	Meghalaya	Meghalaya	7	42
18	Orissa	Odisha		
19	Patna	Bihar	84	1142

S. No.	High Court	State	Court Complexes	Courts
20	Punjab & Haryana	Chandigarh Haryana Punjab	1 53 64	30 500 541
21	Rajasthan	Rajasthan	247	1240
22	Sikkim	Sikkim	8	23
23	Telangana	Telangana	129	476
24	Tripura	Tripura	14	84
25	Uttarakhand	Uttarakhand	69	271

Conclusion

The Economic Survey 2018-19, in a chapter titled 'Ending Matsyanyaya', quotes Kautilya's Arthashastra stating that the rule of law and maintenance of order is the science of governance. It also mentions Kamandak's Nitisara, which emphasises that no branch of knowledge or policy is of any use if the rule of law is neglected. The preamble to the Constitution of India defines the first role of the State as 'to secure for all its citizens: justice, social, economic, and political'. In order for a country to be prosperous, ensure inclusive development, and maintain harmony in society, it is sin qua non that the rule of law is the order of the day. Therefore, for India to achieve its goal of becoming a developed nation by 2047, it needs to have a well-oiled and well-functioning judiciary that is not housed in crowded courtrooms, falling buildings, or crumbling spaces. In the age of machine learning, the judiciary need not be a Remington typewriter; it needs to be sophisticated, tech-savvy, and driven by the zeitgeist of high productivity. Its judges need to have modern courtrooms so they can deliver swift justice because, as famously noted in Shakespeare's *Hamlet*, 'For who would bear the Whips and Scorns of time, The Oppressor's wrong ... the Law's delay' (Chapter 5).

CHAPTER 5

Right to Legal Aid

Vishnu Tiwari spent 20 years of his life in jail in a false rape case waiting for his appeal to be heard by the high court. Finally, in 2021 he was acquitted but had already lost the prime years of his life and was a broken man. Nonetheless, it was a freedom he craved for long, and it became possible only because of the legal aid provided to him by the State Legal Services Authority.

In a country where more than 80 crore people are eligible for free ration, it is not difficult to ascertain the number of people eligible for free legal aid. According to Section 12 of the Legal Services Authorities Act, the following sections of society are eligible for free legal aid:

a) Members of Scheduled Castes or Scheduled Tribes
b) A victim of trafficking in human beings or beggars, as referred to in Article 23 of the Constitution
c) A woman or a child
d) A mentally ill or otherwise disabled person
e) A person under circumstances of undeserved want, such as being a victim of a mass disaster, ethnic violence, caste atrocity, flood, drought, earthquake, or industrial disaster
f) An industrial workman
g) In custody, including custody in a protective home within the meaning of Clause (g) of Section 2 of the Immoral Traffic

(Prevention) Act, 1956 (104 of 1956); or in a juvenile home within the meaning of Clause (j) of Section 2 of the Juvenile Justice Act, 1986 (53 of 1986); or in a psychiatric hospital or psychiatric nursing home within the meaning of Clause (g) of Section 2 of the Mental Health Act, 1987(14 of 1987)

h) A person in receipt of annual income less than the amount mentioned in the following schedule (or any other higher amount as may be prescribed by the State government) if the case is before a court other than the Supreme Court and less than Rs 5 lakh if the case is before the Supreme Court.

In March 2021, *Live Law* reported that Justice N.V. Ramana, the then chief justice of India, said that around 48,227 panel lawyers are empanelled with the Legal Services Authorities throughout India to provide necessary legal services. The Legal Services Authorities have also engaged pro-bono lawyers, which include many senior lawyers. Till now, 3175 pro-bono lawyers have been empanelled at the district level, 437 at the high court level, and 86 at the Supreme Court level.[1]

Different states prescribe different income ceilings for availing of free legal aid. While Mizoram fixed it at Rs 25000, in states like Delhi and Andhra Pradesh, people with an income of less than Rs 3 lakh can avail themselves of free legal aid.[2] According to a report by the Bengaluru-based civil society organisation DAKSH, titled 'Access to Justice' survey, 90 per cent of the litigants earn less than Rs 3 lakh per annum. This means that even in the states with the highest income ceiling, 90 per cent of the litigants are eligible for free legal aid.[3]

United Nations Principles and Guidelines on Access to Legal Aid in Criminal Justice Systems mark 'legal aid as an essential element of a fair, humane, and efficient criminal justice system that is based on the rule of law'. According to the guidelines,

'Legal aid is a foundation for the enjoyment of other rights, including the right to a fair trial, as defined in Article 11, Paragraph 1, of the Universal Declaration of Human Rights, a precondition to exercising such rights and an important safeguard that ensures fundamental fairness and public trust in the criminal justice process.'

The Indian Constitution has also recognised and stressed the importance of legal aid. Article 14 of the Indian Constitution states, 'The State shall not deny to any person equality before the law and the equal protection of the laws within India.' Article 22(1) of the Constitution says that no person who is arrested shall be detained in custody without being informed, as soon as may be, of the grounds for such arrest, nor shall he be denied the right to consult and to be defended by, a legal practitioner of his choice.

Article 39A of the Constitution obligates that the 'State shall secure that the operation of the legal system promotes justice, on the basis of equal opportunity, and shall, in particular, provide free legal aid, by suitable legislation or schemes or in any other way, to ensure that opportunities for securing justice are not denied to any citizen by reason of economic or other disabilities'.

The Legal Services Authorities Act was enacted by Parliament in 1987 to establish a nationwide uniform network for providing free and competent legal services to the weaker sections of society based on equal opportunity. It came into force on 9 November 1995.

According to the Department of Justice, 'The National Legal Services Authority (NALSA) has been constituted under the Legal Services Authorities Act, 1987 to monitor and evaluate the implementation of legal aid programmes and to lay down policies and principles for making legal services available under the Act.'

In every state, a State Legal Services Authority and in every high court, a High Court Legal Services Committee has been constituted. District Legal Services Authorities and Taluk Legal Services Committees have been constituted in districts and most taluks to give effect to the policies and directions of the NALSA and provide free legal services to the people and conduct Lok Adalats in the state.

The Supreme Court Legal Services Committee has been constituted to administer and implement the legal services programme insofar as it relates to the Supreme Court of India. Despite these best of intentions, legal aid in India has been far from satisfactory.

In October 2021, the then executive chairman of the National Legal Services Authority, Justice Uday U. Lalit highlighted a disturbing fact that an 'overwhelming majority of the general public is not utilising the free legal aid services due to many reasons including the lack of awareness and poor quality of the aid offered'.[4]

He said that legal aid to the poor does not mean poor legal aid. He also highlighted an important fact that only 1 per cent of the total criminal cases heard in the courts of law get legal aid from the offices of legal services authorities across the country.

The poor quality of legal aid can be gauged from what the Supreme Court said in a judgment wherein it acquitted a man who was sentenced to death for the alleged murder of his wife and four kids. In *Ramanand @ Nandlal Bharti vs State of Uttar Pradesh*, the apex court noted, 'What is meant by the duty of the State to ensure a fair defence to an accused is not the employment of a defence counsel for namesake. It has to be the provision of a counsel who defends the accused diligently to the best of his abilities. While the quality of the defence or the calibre of the counsel would not militate against the guarantee of a fair trial sanctioned by Articles 21 and 22 of the Constitution, a threshold level of competence and due diligence in the discharge of his duties as a defence counsel would certainly be the constitutional guaranteed expectation. The presence of counsel on record means effective, genuine and faithful presence and not a mere farcical, sham or a virtual presence that is illusory, if not fraudulent.'

Highlighting the poor defence by the defence counsel, the court said,

> Before parting with the case, we would like to place on record an observation of ours, touching an important aspect of the case. Without any hesitation and with disappointment, we state that the case on hand is one of the most perfunctory investigations. It appears that the accused herein was provided with a legal aid. He might not have been able to afford a good and experienced trial lawyer to defend himself. We have noticed that the cross-examination of each and every witness is below average. Questions which the defence counsel was not supposed to put to the prosecution witnesses were put without realizing or understanding the legal implications of the answers to such questions, more particularly, when they were not necessary. The defence counsel remained oblivious of the position of law that suggestions made to the witnesses by the defence the answers to those are binding to the accused.

According to the 'Access to Justice' 2016, 90 per cent of the litigants earn less than Rs 3 lakh per annum. When this data is put in the context of the fact that only 1 per cent of the total criminal cases heard in the courts of law get legal aid from the offices of Legal Services Authorities across the country, the conclusion one can derive is that even people earning less than Rs 3 lakh per annum do not avail the free legal aid.

Justice Lalit raised an important question that leaves the stakeholders with a valid point of introspection. He said,

> Is it that the remaining 99 per cent of the general public does not want legal aid? There could be two reasons why people do not receive legal aid. First, many people are not aware that it is their constitutional right to be provided free legal aid. Second, they may lack confidence in the legal aid system, which is more dangerous. If they do not have confidence in the setup or in the machinery of legal aid, then we need to do self-introspection. Good quality aid must be ensured. Legal aid to the poor does not mean poor legal aid. There has to be better standard, better quality and better level of legal aid offered through legal services authorities.

The *Death Penalty India Report,* released by the Centre of Death Penalty at National Law University, Delhi, in May 2016, made an observation that has a significant bearing on legal aid. The report noted,

> Very often, the concern about the quality of legal representation has been couched in terms of inadequacies of the legal aid system. More than 60 per cent of the prisoners sentenced to death had private lawyers in the trial court and high courts. It must be a cause for extreme concern that prisoners and their families wanted to avoid the legal aid system at all costs and therefore went to great lengths to ensure that they had private legal representation.

The inadequacies of the legal aid system in India have pushed millions of litigants—the majority of which belongs to the economically weaker section (a fact highlighted in various reports)—to hire 'expensive' courtroom heroes, making justice impossible for many.

According to *India Justice Report 2019,* almost 80 per cent of India's population is eligible for free legal aid. Yet since 1995, barely 15 million people have been provided legal services and advice by legal services institutions (LSI) established all across the country under the Legal Services Authorities Act, 1987. The department-related parliamentary standing committee (DPRSC) on personal, public grievances, law and justice observed in its 116th report the same problem. It stated, 'The majority of Indians are eligible to receive legal aid, but the number of people actually receiving legal aid is a minuscule percentage of those entitled.'

There are several reasons for the poor state of legal aid in India. One of the reasons is poor funding. According to the *India Justice Report 2022*, the national per capita spending on legal aid, including the expenditure of the NALSA and the state/UT governments themselves, is a 'meagre Rs 4.57 per annum'. Excluding NALSA, this figure drops to Rs 3.84, and if only NALSA's budget (2021–22) is considered, the per capita spend is Rs 0.73 paise only.[5]

The *India Justice Report 2022* made another important observation in relation to the legal aid clinics that are supposed to provide legal counselling, referral, and representational and awareness services in areas where people face 'geographical, social, and other barriers'. The report stated that between March 2020 and March 2022, legal aid clinics across India's nearly 6 lakh villages reduced by 66.6 per cent–from 14,159 to 4723. This meant the national average for villages per legal aid clinic went up from 42 to 127. Most states and union territories recorded a decline in the number of legal service clinics across villages.[6]

As mentioned earlier, NALSA is the central body that provides legal aid. The states also contribute finances towards providing free legal aid. According to the *India Justice Report 2022*, between 2020 and 2022, the overall allocation for legal services increased substantially. NALSA's disbursement to states increased by 46 per cent to 144.3 crore in 2021–23 (from Rs 99 crore in 2020–21). For the most part, state contributions to the legal aid budgets also increased. For example, in 2019–20, the Haryana government contributed 68 per cent to the total legal aid budget and the remaining 32 per cent came from NALSA. In 2021–22,

Haryana's state share shot up to 83 per cent, with only Rs 6.5 crore (65 million) being provided by NALSA to the total legal aid budget of Rs 38.6 crore (386 million).

The report highlights an important fact concerning the state's funding for free legal aid. According to the report,

> Historically, state spending on legal aid has been uneven and low. In 2017–18, six states/union territories had not contributed towards legal services at all. As of 2021–22, all states/union territories had contributed towards their legal aid budgets. The increased willingness to contribute suggests two things: growing awareness of and demand for legal aid, which must be met, and an increasing recognition of the value of providing better and more widely spread legal services. Except for Nagaland and Chandigarh, all states/union territories contributed more than 60 per cent to their legal aid budgets. Four states–Goa, Madhya Pradesh, Sikkim, and Uttar Pradesh–contributed more than 90 per cent. Allocations by Assam, Andhra Pradesh, Rajasthan, and Telangana reduced marginally.

The report also states that the overall utilisation of NALSA funds reduced in 2021–22. Of the Rs 183 crore (1.83 billion) allotted to states, Rs 138 crore (1.38 billion) remained unutilised. Only Jharkhand and Manipur utilised 100 per cent, followed by Arunachal Pradesh and Mizoram (97 per cent each), while Odisha and Andhra Pradesh could manage only 50 per cent. Goa with 49 per cent utilised the least. The fact that funds remained unutilised comes as a surprise because most of the legal aid lawyers complain of low payment.

According to an IndiaSpend report, low pay is one of the biggest reasons behind the lack of good resources. The legal aid lawyers IndiaSpend spoke to said that there is little incentive to be part of the legal aid system as 'pay is not commensurate with the work or the effort it took them to become a lawyer, payments from the legal aid services authority are often delayed, legal aid counsel are not respected as much as private lawyers in court, and they do not get any social security benefits as they are not employees'.[7]

According to the report, Jeet Mann Singh, a professor of legal education and research at the National Law University in Delhi, said, 'If lawyers will not be paid well, why will a competent lawyer empanel themselves as a panel lawyer/free legal aid counsel? Thus, the quality of the service keeps deteriorating.'

According to the Ministry of Justice, 9.75 lakh people have been provided with free legal services from April 2022 to January 2023. A sum of Rs 200 crore in the budget estimates during the financial year 2023/24 was allocated to NALSA.[8]

In August 2022, Justice Lalit, the then chief justice of India-designate and executive chairman of NALSA, made a remark that poses an important challenge to the government aiming to ensure free legal aid to the poor. Justice Lalit said that over 70 per cent of the population is below the poverty line and only 12 per cent opt for free legal aid provided by legal services authorities.[9]

He then posed an important question that had a very uncomfortable answer. 'What does the population between 12 and 70 per cent do?' he said. He added, 'That means the difference between 12 per cent and 70 per cent is not with us. They have solicited the engagement of private counsel...They must have sold their assets; they must have sold their jewellery; they must have mortgaged their properties; that is what the litigation brings in. Litigation is like a bleeding wound. The more you let it bleed, the more will the man suffer.'[10]

According to a paper by NALSA on the Legal Aid Defense Counsel Scheme 2022, at present the assigned counsel system of dispensation of legal aid is being followed in India. Under the said system, cases are assigned to panel lawyers by legal services institutions. Such panel lawyers to whom cases are assigned, also have private practices, and hence, they do not exclusively devote their time to the legal aid matters. Many times, their accessibility and availability remain an issue for timely client consultation and updating the legal aid seekers about the progress of their cases. There have been a few instances wherein the lawyers were found harassing beneficiaries or demanding fees from them.[11]

To improve the quality of legal aid services, taking certain steps to strengthen court-based legal services is necessary. One such important step in this regard is adopting another legal aid delivery-based model called the 'Legal Aid Defense Counsel System'. This system will provide legal aid in criminal matters along the lines of the public defender system on a pilot basis for a period of two years. Under this system, the legal aid lawyers will exclusively deal with legal aided cases.

In November 2023, during the first regional conference on Access to Legal Aid, organised by NALSA in collaboration with the International Legal Foundation (ILF), UNDP, and UNICEF, Attorney General R. Venkatraman made a pertinent point when he said that lawyers should consider participation in legal aid services not just as a professional duty but as an ethical and moral dimension of their profession.

In a country with a vast population living below the poverty line, free legal aid cannot be a matter of choice but an obligation on the part of the government. While lawyers can be motivated to treat legal aid as a moral dimension of their profession, this noble vision cannot be attained unless there are good incentives in terms of money and recognition for lawyers willing to work as legal aid providers.

CHAPTER 6

Public Interest Litigation

On 15 November 1977, the Ministry of Home Affairs, Government of India, constituted the National Police Commission to 'study the problems of police and make a comprehensive review of the police system at national level'.[1]

One of its members, K.F. Rustamji, former IGP of Madhya Pradesh and ex-special secretary to the Ministry of Home, visited the jails in Bihar and wrote about the conditions of the undertrials who were languishing for long periods. He wrote a series of articles highlighting the plight of undertrials, which were published in *The Indian Express* in January 1979. One of these articles caught the attention of a Supreme Court lawyer Pushpa Kapila Hingorani. Hingorani was moved by the plight of this undertrial and decided to intervene. She filed a *Habeas Corpus* petition in the Supreme Court of India, in which she named nineteen undertrials mentioned in Rustamji's article as the petitioners. One of them was a Bangladeshi immigrant named Hussainara Khatoon, whose name would occupy the title of the case.

The travesty of justice can be gauged from the fact that many of the prisoners had been in jail awaiting trial for periods much longer than the actual punishment awardable for their alleged crimes. For example, one of the prisoners who had spent over eight years in jail was accused of an offence punishable with a maximum term of two years.

Acting on Hingorani's petition, the Supreme Court ordered the release of the undertrial prisoners and made scathing remarks against the Bihar government. Justice P.N. Bhagwati wrote in his judgment that the petition discloses a shocking state of affairs regarding the administration of justice in Bihar. 'An alarmingly large number of men and women, including children, are behind prison bars for years awaiting trial in courts of law. The offences with which some of them are charged are trivial, which, even if proved, would not warrant punishment for more than a few months, perhaps for a year or two, and yet these unfortunate forgotten specimens of humanity are in jail, deprived of their freedom, for periods ranging from three to ten years without even as much as their trial having commenced. It is a crying shame on the judicial system which permits incarceration of men and women for such long periods of time without trial,' read the judgment.

The apex court held a speedy trial as a fundamental right within the scope of Article 21. After the petition of Hingorani, the Supreme Court took up such cases and issued guidelines to ensure speedy trials of those languishing in jails and ordered the release of 40,000 undertrial prisoners across the country. Since then, public interest litigations (PILs) have become a widely used mechanism to address issues of social, economic, and political significance.

PIL became a means to seek justice for those who could not do it for themselves. Moreover, a PIL became an effective means of securing justice for the poor and marginalised, apart from addressing important political and social issues.

The case was a marked departure from the tradition because Hingorani was in no manner related directly to the petitioner.

Nevertheless, her petition was accepted by the apex court. Kapila Hingorani was permitted to pursue a case in which she had no 'locus standi' after considering the fact that her petition involved a matter of 'public interest'. Her plea was heard by Justice P.N. Bhagwati who along with Justice V.R. Krishna Iyer is credited with pioneering PIL in India. Since then, the 'locus standi' of the petitioner has not become a hurdle in seeking justice for a wrong committed.

While the genesis of PIL can be traced to a case titled *Mumbai Kamagar Sabha vs Abdul Thai*, it was the Hussainara Khatoon case that established PIL as an effective mechanism to address important issues. It has been used to address major social, political, economic, and environmental issues.

In 1982, Bandhua Mukti Morcha, a non-governmental organisation (NGO) dedicated to the cause of forced and bonded labourers in the country, wrote to Justice P.N. Bhagwati alleging that a large number of labourers from different parts of the country were working under inhuman and intolerable conditions in some of the stone quarries located in Faridabad, Haryana. It also said that a large number of these were bonded labourers.

The petitioner requested the issuance of a writ petition to ensure the proper implementation of labour welfare laws such as the Mines Act of 1952, the Inter-State Migrant Workmen (Regulation of Employment and Conditions of Service) Act 1979, the Contract Labour (Regulation and Abolition) Act 1970, the Bonded Labour System (Abolition) Act 1976, and the Minimum Wages Act of 1948, among others. The court treated the letter as a writ petition and appointed a commission consisting of two lawyers to inquire into the allegations made by the petitioner. The Commission verified and confirmed the allegations made by the NGO and pointed out in its report that:

i. the whole atmosphere in the alleged stone quarries was full of dust and it was difficult for anyone to breathe
ii. some of the workers were not allowed to leave the stone quarries and were providing forced labour
iii. there was no facility of providing clean water to drink, and the labourers were compelled to drink dirty water from a nullah
iv. the labourers did not have proper shelter and were living in jhuggis with stones piled one upon the other as walls and straw covering the top which made the roof too low to stand and did not provide any protection against sun and rain
v. some of the labourers suffered from chronic diseases
vi. no compensation was being paid to labourers who were injured due to accidents arising in the course of employment
vii. there were no facilities for medical treatment.

One of the issues involved in the case was whether a letter personally addressed to a judge could be considered as a writ petition. On this, the court held,

> Where a member of the public acting bona fide moves the court for enforcement of a fundamental right on behalf of a person or class of persons who on account of poverty or disability or socially or economically disadvantaged position cannot approach the court for relief, such member of the public may move the court even by just writing a letter, because it would not be right or fair to expect a person acting pro bono publico to incur expenses out of his own pocket for going to a lawyer and preparing a regular writ petition for being filed in court for enforcement of the fundamental right of the poor and deprived sections of the community and in such a case, a letter addressed by him can legitimately be regarded as an 'appropriate' proceeding.

The court further made a very important observation regarding the utility of PIL. It held,

> Public interest litigation is not in the nature of adversary litigation but it is a challenge and an opportunity to the government and its officers to make basic human rights meaningful to the deprived and vulnerable sections of the community and to assure them of social and economic justice which is the signature tune of our Constitution. When the court entertains PIL, it does not do so in a cavilling spirit or in a confrontational mood or with a view to tilting at executive authority or seeking to usurp it, but its attempt is only to ensure observance of social and economic rescue programmes, legislative as well as executive, framed for the benefit of the have-nots and the handicapped and to protect them against violation of their basic human rights, which is also the constitutional obligation of the executive.

The court issued several directions to the Haryana government and central government to ensure proper remedies for the aggrieved. These directions included the constitution of a vigilance committee in each division of the district to ensure compliance under Section 13 of the Bonded Labour Act, 1976, and rehabilitation of the bonded labourers.

In the last forty-five years, the Supreme Court through PIL has expanded the ambit and scope of fundamental rights and, at the same time, expanded the scope of its powers to enforce the same.

In the case of *S.P. Gupta vs Union of India*, it was established that if a specific class of people's legal rights have been violated and they are unable to approach the court for relief due to their poverty, helplessness, disability, socially or economically disadvantaged position, then any member of the public can maintain an application in the high court under Article 226. In the case of breach of any fundamental right of such person, the application can be filed in the court under Article 32 to seek judicial redress for the legal wrong or injury caused to them.

Justice Bhagwati further said in the judgment, 'Whenever there is public wrong or public injury caused by omission or act or omission of the State or by a public authority which is contrary to the constitution or law, any member acting bona fide and having sufficient interest can maintain such action for redressal of such wrong or public injury.'

PIL acquired a new meaning and dimension with the landmark decision in *Sunil Batra vs Delhi Administration*. This new dimension was called 'epistolary jurisdiction'. In this case, while accepting a letter by a jail inmate who alleged torture by the jail warden on a fellow inmate, the court held,

> Technicalities and legal niceties are no impediment to the court entertaining even an informal communication as a proceeding for habeas corpus if the basic facts are found; still, the awe and distance of courts, the legalese and mystique, keep the institution unapproachable. More realistic is to devise a method of taking the healing law to the injured victim. That system is best where the remedy will rush to the injury on the slightest summons. So, within the existing, dated legislation, new meanings must be read. Of course, new legislation is the best solution, but when lawmakers take far too long for social patience to suffer, as in this very case of prison reform, courts have to make-do with interpretation and carve on wood and sculpt on stone ready at hand and not wait for far away marble architecture.

The Supreme Court has repeatedly emphasised the importance of PIL for securing justice for those unable to seek it themselves. From passing directions to the effect of making it obligatory for a doctor or a hospital, both public and private, to provide immediate medical aid to a victim of a road accident to decriminalising consensual sex, all have been the result of a PIL.

Pandit Paramanad Katara, a senior advocate and human rights activist, filed a writ petition in the public interest based on a newspaper report concerning the death of a scooterist knocked down by a speeding car. The report said that despite the injured person being taken to the nearest hospital, the doctors refused to attend to him. The hospital said that the accident victim should be taken to another hospital located 20 km away, which was authorised to handle medico-legal cases. The victim succumbed to his injuries before he could be taken to the other hospital.

Katara prayed the directions be issued to the Union of India that every injured citizen brought for treatment should instantaneously be given medical aid to preserve life. The court made two critical observations and directions:

1. Every doctor at a government hospital or otherwise has the professional obligation to extend their services with due expertise for protecting life. No law or state action can intervene to avoid/delay in the discharge of this paramount obligation cast upon the members of the medical profession. The obligation being total, absolute, and paramount, laws of procedure, whether in statutes or otherwise, which would interfere with the discharge of this obligation cannot be sustained and must, therefore, give way.
2. We would also like to mention that whenever on such occasion a man of the medical profession is approached, and if he finds that whatever assistance he could give is not sufficient really to save the life of the person but, some better assistance is necessary, it is the duty of the man in the medical profession so approached to render all the help which he could and also see that the person reaches the proper expert as early as possible.

It was a PIL filed by the Naz Foundation that led to the decriminalisation of homosexuality. In 2018, the Supreme

Court of India, with a stroke of a judgment, restored 'inclusiveness' by decriminalising part of Section 377 that made consensual sex between consenting homosexuals a crime.

The Supreme Court, in its judgment, said,

> An examination of Section 377 IPC on the anvil of Article 19(1)(a) reveals that it amounts to an unreasonable restriction, for public decency and morality cannot be amplified beyond a rational or logical limit and cannot be accepted as reasonable grounds for curbing the fundamental rights of freedom of expression and choice of the LGBTQ community. Consensual carnal intercourse among adults, be it homosexual or heterosexual, in private space, does not in any way harm the public decency or morality. Therefore, Section 377 IPC in its present form violates Article 19(1)(a) of the Constitution.

Another landmark judgment that arose out of a PIL was *Vishaka vs the State of Rajasthan*. The trigger of this PIL was the rape of Bhanwari Devi, a social worker in Rajasthan. Bhanwari Devi was part of a Sathin programme that tried to deter people from getting their young children married at a very young age. Bhanwari Devi tried to stop one such marriage, which resulted in her being harassed and boycotted by the villagers and eventually raped by five men in the presence of her husband.

The trial court in Rajasthan acquitted all five men. The acquittal led to the filing of a PIL in the Supreme Court 'seeking detailed directions on how sexual harassment of women at the workplace could be prevented through the judicial process'.[2] The Supreme Court issued certain guidelines to be strictly observed in all workplaces (whether in the private or public sector) and would be 'binding and enforceable in law' until suitable laws were made on the issue.

Zia Mody in her book *10 Judgments That Changed India*[3] enunciates these guidelines:

- The employer and/or other responsible people in a workplace are duty-bound to prevent or deter sexual harassment and set up processes to resolve, settle, or prosecute in such cases.
- For the first time in India, 'sexual harassment' was defined authoritatively. The Supreme Court stated that it includes 'such unwelcome sexually determined behaviour (whether directly or by implication) such as: physical contact and advances, a demand or request for sexual favours, sexually coloured remarks, showing pornography, and any other unwelcome physical, verbal or non-verbal conduct of sexual nature'.
- All employers or persons in charge of workplaces must strive to prevent sexual harassment and, if any act amounts to a specific offence under the Indian Penal Code, 186014 (the IPC) or any other law, they must take appropriate action to punish the guilty.
- Even if the act is not considered a legal offence or a breach of service rules, the employer should create appropriate mechanisms so that the complaint is addressed and redressed in a time-bound manner.
- This complaint mechanism must, if necessary, provide a complaints committee, a special counsellor or other support service, such as assuring confidentiality. The complaints committee should be headed by a woman, and at least half its members must be women. Also, to pre-empt any undue pressure from senior levels, the complaints committee must involve a third party (such as an NGO) familiar with the challenges of sexual harassment.
- The employer must sensitise female employees to their rights and prominently notify the court's guidelines.

- Even if a third party is responsible for sexual harassment, the employer must take all steps necessary to support the victim.
- The central and state governments should adopt suitable measures to ensure that private sector employers implement the guidelines.

Zia Mody writes in her book that 'some authors have correctly observed that Vishaka has institutionalised judicial lawmaking. Whether it has done so or not can be a matter of debate but what cannot be contested is that it led to judicial activism and what Professor Upendra Baxi, one of India's foremost legal scholars, calls it advent of Social Action Litigation'.

PIL has played an important role in securing justice for the unheard. 'Front and centre, PIL now occupies an unrivalled space in Indian constitutional law that bridges the citizen, the court, and the State. It arose in response to citizens seeking to curb widespread human rights violations or illegalities in government functioning that harmed public administration and the environment.'[4]

In the last four decades, the Supreme Court and the respective high courts passed several landmark judgments while hearing PILs that expanded the meaning and scope of the right to life and liberty, equality, and the freedoms guaranteed to the citizens under part three of the Indian Constitution that contains fundamental rights. From addressing environmental issues to issues of women's rights, from ensuring the right to education for children to ensuring the right to live with dignity, PILs have done it all.

However, recent years have seen a spate of cases where PILs have been found to have been filed on most frivolous grounds, sometimes with the aim of gaining publicity, sometimes for private benefit, and sometimes for political reasons. What started as a tool for redressing the grievances of the poor and marginalised gradually became a subject of abuse. It was gradually put to use for private aggrandisement, political purposes, and publicity stunts. There have been several instances when the court has rejected the so-called PILs by discerning an oblique motive of serving a private interest.

On 17 July 2023, the Supreme Court dismissed a PIL that sought an additional stop for the Vande Bharat train. While refusing to entertain the plea, the bench comprising Chief Justice D.Y. Chandrachud, Justice P.S. Narasimha, and Justice Manoj Misra said that the decision to provide stoppages for a train fell under the policy domain of the executive. Hence, the court would not intervene in this matter. Earlier, on 28 April 2023, a division bench of the Kerala High Court too dismissed the same petition categorically stating that there was 'no public interest espoused in the petition'.

Filing such PILs is nothing new. Many frivolous PILs are filed in various courts across the country, which, on the one hand, wastes the precious time of courts that are grappling with huge backlogs and, on the other hand, undermines the credibility of PILs as a mechanism to address important issues.

Commenting on this trend, eminent jurist and former attorney-general of India Soli Sorabjee told the author in 2016,

> Public interest litigation (PIL) is a valuable mechanism to redress the problems of the neglected, alienated and marginalized sections of society. Now, one prerequisite is that it must be instituted "bona fide" and must avoid the three pitfalls associated with PIL: namely 'private interest litigation', 'political interest litigation' and 'publicity interest litigation'. In a way the Supreme Court has itself brought upon itself the problem by entertaining PILs very liberally, if I may say, extravagantly. Every matter of public interest cannot be a matter of public interest litigation. For example, rise in the price of onions. So public interest litigation requires a good jockey in the saddle to keep it on the right track and fulfil the objectives for which it was originally designed.

The Supreme Court had, in many cases, imposed costs and admonished the petitioners who were found to have filed the PILs on frivolous ground or with ulterior motives. In July 2017, sending a stern message to those resorting to the misuse of PILs, the apex court slapped a cost of Rs 25 lakh on an activist for filing a PIL challenging the shifting of the mini-Vidhan Sabha in the Gulbarga district of Karnataka.

The bench of Justice Dipak Misra and Justice A.M. Khanwilkar while imposing the cost said that the petition was 'an abuse of the concept of public interest litigation as it does not espouse any kind of public cause'.

Similarly, in 2018, the Supreme Court imposed a cost of Rs 25,000 on a lawyer named Ashok Pandey who had filed a PIL that sought to reduce the marriageable age for men to 18 years from 21 years. While dismissing the plea and imposing the cost, the bench led by the then chief justice of India Ranjan Gogoi said, 'Wait till an 18-year-old boy moves SC seeking permission to marry.'

And on 4 July 2023, the bench of Chief Justice D.Y. Chandrachud and Justice P.S. Narasimha imposed a cost of Rs 50,000 on a petitioner who had filed two PILs. In the first PIL, the petitioner, an advocate, prayed for a direction to be issued to the union government to 'formulate a policy for reclassification of the caste system' and in the second PIL, he sought a direction to the states and union territories to 'gradually phase out the reservation policy' in public sector employment.

Advocate M.L. Sharma, known as 'serial PIL filer', has faced the ire of the courts many times, and courts have imposed costs on him on several occasions.

In 2016, in an interview with the author, when asked what the way is to prevent the misuse of PILs, Soli Sorabjee said, 'If the court authoritatively declares that it will interfere only in cases of violation of fundamental rights related to people who cannot themselves approach the court because of poverty and lack of resources then it serves a good purpose. The problem is that public interest litigation is indiscriminately resorted to. While it can be misused, it is up to judges to see that it is not. I feel judges sometimes want publicity, to see their names in paper and so entertain sensational PILs.'[5]

As of 1 June 2023, the number of pending matters before the Supreme Court was 68,745, and before the high courts, it was 60.9 lakh. Out of 4.38 crore cases before the lower courts, a considerable number will go to high courts and the Supreme Court as appeals once they are decided. In such a context, the higher judiciary, which is entrusted with hearing constitutional cases of great importance, also cannot afford to waste a single minute on frivolous pleas. Apart from that PIL is a response to the needs of society and has helped in massive social transformation. And, its misuse only dents its credibility, which is not good for our justice system.

CHAPTER 7

The Hope: Alternative Dispute Redressal

The Indian judicial system is grappling with huge pendency and a backlog of cases, which is choking the system. Despite five crore cases pending before different courts, new ones are being instituted every day. The National Judicial Data Grid reported that in November 2023, 1,446,750 new cases were instituted and 977,402 were disposed of, indicating that the backlog is not decreasing but only increasing as the number of cases instituted is higher than those disposed of. The Indian courts are clogged with long, unsettled cases.

The issue of a considerable backlog is much debated, and often mind-boggling numbers are put forward highlighting the not-so-positive future that the judiciary is staring at. In 2010, Andhra Pradesh High Court Judge V.V. Rao said it would take 320 years to clear backlog cases. According to a NITI Aayog strategy paper of 2018, at the current rate of disposal of cases in Indian courts, it will take over 324 years to clear the backlog. Retired Supreme Court Judge Markandey Katju was slightly more pessimistic, estimating that it will take about 360 years to clear the backlog of cases if no new cases are filed. Since these estimates were made, the number of pending cases has increased substantially, while the number of judges has only increased marginally. In such a scenario, a system of Alternative Dispute Resolution (ADR) becomes not only an option but an indispensable choice. Section 89 of the Civil Procedure Code provides for the settlement of disputes outside the court.

Clause 1 of Section 89 of the Civil Procedure Code says that where it appears to the court that there exist elements of a settlement that may be acceptable to the parties, the court shall formulate the terms of settlement and give them to the parties for their observations and after receiving the observations of the parties, the court may reformulate the terms of a possible settlement and refer the same for the following:

a) Arbitration
b) Conciliation
c) Judicial settlement, including settlement through Lok Adalat
d) Mediation

Clause 2 states that where a dispute has been referred

a) for arbitration or conciliation, the provisions of the Arbitration and Conciliation Act, 1996 (26 of 1996) shall apply as if the proceedings for arbitration or conciliation were referred for settlement under the provisions of that Act;
b) to Lok Adalat, the court shall refer the same to the Lok Adalat in accordance with the provisions of sub-section (1) of Section 20 of the Legal Services Authority Act, 1987 (39 of 1987) and all other provisions of that Act shall apply in respect of the dispute so referred to the Lok Adalat;
c) for judicial settlement, the court shall refer the same to a suitable institution or person and such institution or person shall be deemed to be a Lok Adalat and all the provisions of the Legal Services Authority Act, 1987 (39 of 1987) shall

apply as if the dispute were referred to a Lok Adalat under the provisions of that Act;

d) for mediation, the court shall affect a compromise between the parties and shall follow such procedure as may be prescribed.

According to the Ministry of Law and Justice, alternate dispute resolution methods have been promoted 'wholeheartedly'. An important step taken in this direction was the amendment of the Commercial Courts Act, 2015, on 20 August 2018, making pre-institution mediation and settlement (PIMS) mandatory in the case of commercial disputes. Amendment to the Arbitration and Conciliation Act, 1996 has been made by the Arbitration and Conciliation (Amendment) Act 2015 to expedite the speedy resolution of disputes by prescribing timelines.[1]

One of the most important and widely accepted and used mechanisms of alternate dispute resolution is the functioning of Lok Adalats. According to the Ministry of Law and Justice, a Lok Adalat is an important alternative dispute resolution mechanism available to common people. It is a forum where the disputes/cases pending in the court of law or at the pre-litigation stage are settled/compromised amicably.

Under the Legal Services Authorities (LSA) Act, 1987, an award made by a Lok Adalat is deemed to be a decree of a civil court and is final and binding on all parties, and no appeal lies against thereto before any court. A Lok Adalat is not a permanent establishment and national Lok Adalats are organised simultaneously in all taluks, districts, and high courts on a pre-fixed date.

The Ministry of Law and Justice in 2022 referred to the emergence of Lok Adalat as the most efficacious tool of Alternative Dispute Resolution. In 2021, a total of 12,787,329 cases were resolved and with technological advancements, such as E-Lok Adalats, Lok Adalats have reached the doorsteps of parties.

Lok Adalats have proved to be an effective mechanism and platform for settling long pending disputes. In July 2023, at the national-level Lok Adalat, a sixty-three-year-old civil dispute pending in the court of principal civil judge, Hubballi and a forty-one-year-old suit pending in the Gadag district court were successfully settled.[2]

The scope and effectiveness of Lok Adalats in settling disputes can be gauged by the fact that during the first National Lok Adalat held in February 2023, over 97.64 lakh pending (17.13 lakh) and pre-litigation (80.5 lakh) cases were settled. At the fourth National Lok Adalat, held on 9 December 2023, 11,743,465 cases were resolved, including 1,198,278 pending cases and 10,545,187 pre-litigation cases. The approximate value of the total settlement amount in these cases was Rs 20,510 crore.

The details of the case disposed of in Lok Adalats during the last three years are tabulated here.

Years	Pre-litigation Cases	Pending Cases	Grand Total
2021	7,206,294	5,581,743	12,788,037
2022	31,015,215	10,910,795	41,926,010
2023 (up to 17 Jun 2023)	30,011,291	6,188,686	36,199,977
Total	68,232,800	22,681,224	90,914,024

In December 2022, Kiren Rijiju, the then law minister, highlighted the importance of Lok Adalat. In a written reply to a question in the Lok Sabha, he said that Lok Adalat is primarily a 'People's Court' wherein decisions are arrived at between two or more disputing parties on mutually acceptable terms amicably.

To reduce the pendency of cases in courts and also to settle disputes at the pre-litigation stage, Lok Adalats are organised by Legal Services Institutions at such intervals as they deem fit.[3]

According to a report by *The Hindu*, in 2020, a daily wager named Jitendra Kumar Sethy in Odisha's Kandhamal district moved the Lok Adalat against Prime Minister Narendra Modi after allegedly failing to get an Aadhaar card registered in his name despite 21 attempts. Jitendra Kumar Sethy said, 'I need not have to spend anything for fighting my case. I decided to sue the Prime Minister as he is the one who is responsible for the implementation of Aadhaar.' We do not have to go into the specifics of the case, but we can and should appreciate the Lok Adalats in getting accessibility to a common person.[4]

The resolution of cases at Lok Adalats helps litigants avoid the costs and delays associated with the court-based justice system and reduces the pendency of cases in the courts.

Justice Sanjay Kishan Kaul, Judge, Supreme Court of India, and Executive Chairman, NALSA, supervised the fourth National Lok Adalat and made an important point. He said, 'The swift resolution of cases at Lok Adalats will alleviate the immense pressure on the court system, allowing judges to dedicate their valuable time and resources to more complex and urgent issues.'

Although Lok Adalats has been functioning for forty years, there are still some issues that need to be addressed. In one of his articles published in *The Hindu* in 2021, legal scholar Faizan Mustafa posed some very apt and relevant questions that require attention. He said, 'Do they empower the poor or coerce them to accept unjust compromises? Do they trade justice off for high settlement numbers and speed, ignoring the old dictum that justice hurried is justice buried? Have we tailored a dual system of justice dispensation, where the formal legal system, i.e., the court, is meant only for the rich and powerful?'[5]

In *State of Punjab & Anr vs Jalour Singh & Ors* on 18 January 2008, the Supreme Court held,

> Every Lok Adalat shall, while determining any reference before it under this Act, act with utmost expedition to arrive at a compromise or settlement between the parties and shall be guided by the principles of justice, equity, fair play, and other legal principles. It is evident from the said provisions that Lok Adalats have no adjudicatory or judicial functions. Their functions relate purely to conciliation. A Lok Adalat determines a reference on the basis of a compromise or settlement between the parties at its instance, and put its seal of confirmation by making an award in terms of the compromise or settlement. When the Lok Adalat is not able to arrive at a settlement or compromise, no award is made and the case record is returned to the court from which the reference was received, for disposal in accordance with law. No Lok Adalat has the power to "hear" parties to adjudicate cases as a court does. It discusses the subject matter with the parties and persuades them to arrive at a just settlement. In their conciliatory role, the Lok Adalats are guided by principles of justice, equity, fair play.

In *New Okhla Industrial Development vs Yunus*, the Supreme Court on 3 February 2022 further held that 'an award passed by the Lok Adalat under 1987 Act is the culmination of a non-adjudicatory process. The parties are persuaded even by members of the Lok Adalat to arrive at mutually agreeable compromise'.

The principles of justice serve as the guiding force for Lok Adalats. However, sometimes these principles are overlooked in order to be swift and efficient. This compromise at the end of the case is not out of free choice but rather imposed on the poor. American political philosopher Michael Sandel argues that a contract is valid only when autonomy and reciprocity are present in it in its truest sense. Unfortunately, both these elements are sometimes missing from the Lok Adalats decisions or 'settlements'.

Faizan Mustafa in the aforementioned article has mentioned how, in most cases, litigants simply want to end the long pending cases and have to accept discounted future values of their claims instead of their just entitlements or small compensations. He also said, 'Poor women under the so-called "harmony ideology" of the state are virtually dictated by family courts to compromise matrimonial disputes under a romanticised view of marriage. Even a disaster like the Bhopal gas tragedy was coercively settled for a paltry sum, with real justice still eluding thousands of victims.'

Considering all these issues, it becomes imperative to craft some creative solutions to ensure that 'settlements' are not imposed on the people who have no way out for the sake of swiftness. Rather 'justice' must occur and it must be qualitative.

Conclusion

Ram Swarup, a resident of Lohar Majra village located in Pehowa tehsil of Kurukshetra district in Haryana, lost his daughter in 1993 who was raped and murdered. The tragedy of losing a daughter was met with another tragedy. Swarup was accused of raping and murdering his daughter. He spent nearly two years in jail before being acquitted by the trial court in 1997. Though he was acquitted, the stigma of being accused of raping and murdering his daughter never left him.

Even the acquittal would not have been possible had it not been for a social worker Sudesh Kumari who moved the high court for a CBI inquiry. On the court's order in 1996, the CBI took over the case and found that police had falsely implicated Ram Swarup. The CBI found Swarup was implicated falsely by the investigating officer and a senior police official in connivance with people with 'high political connections' who were interested in protecting the suspects. The high court observed, 'The facts and the circumstances of this case have proved beyond doubt that the investigation in the case was not properly conducted and completed. The approach adopted by the investigation agency was casual and not specific. Efforts were made to shield the real culprits. The respondent agencies are proved to have been aware of the facts that persons other than the father of the deceased were responsible for the commission of the crime.'

The court found that it was a fit case where it should exercise the discretion to do complete justice to order a CBI investigation and the mere conviction or acquittal of Ram Sarup would not by itself be sufficient. The court observed, 'It is in the interest of the State and the general public that the matter should be thoroughly proved, inquired and investigated by an independent agency.'

Extra-judicial confession based on which the prosecution had proceeded with the case was retracted. The CBI also found that the scientific lab reports showed that the semen stains found on the undergarments of the deceased did not match the DNA test done on the petitioner. It also found that the recovery memos of the alleged weapon used for murder had been falsely created with the aid of two witnesses. While Swarup's innocence was approved by the trial court and the high court, his life had been destroyed.

To compensate in some manner for the ordeal faced by Swarup, Sudesh Kumari moved the high court in May 1999. She sought compensation for Swaroop for violation of liberty and dignity and being 'maliciously prosecuted for an offence of rape against his own daughter'.

When sixteen years later, on 9 February 2015, the Punjab and Haryana High Court ordered a compensation of Rs 5 lakh to Ram Swarup, a flicker of justice was seen. But the tragedy ended in a bigger tragedy. Neither Ram Swarup nor his wife Javitri, who worked as farm labourers, were alive to receive the compensation. Ram Sarup died in 2008 and his wife in 2009.

The Constitution of India guarantees against double jeopardy. Article 20(2) of the Constitution of India states, 'No person shall be prosecuted and punished for the same offence more than once.' But when the process itself becomes a punishment, one is punished for an offence multiple times and sometimes one has to bear the wrath of the punishing state without an offence.

The fact that Ram Swarup's daughter was murdered was the failure of the state to protect its citizens. It could have been corrected in some measure by punishing the guilty. The fact that those guilty went scot-free was the failure of the law. But the biggest failure was that of the criminal justice system, which could not compensate Swarup for the wrongs committed to him in his lifetime.

It is said that law is born from the despair of human nature. But 'justice is the sum of all moral duty'. A state or society that fails to ensure justice to its populace fails morally.

In numerous cases, respective high courts and the Supreme Court have delved into the issue of equal access to justice. In July 2022, granting relief to five *jhuggi* dwellers in Delhi, the Delhi High Court said, 'Law, with all its legalese, is worth tinsel, if the underprivileged cannot get justice. At the end of the day, our preambular goal is not law but justice. Law is but the instrument, the via media, as it were, to attain the ultimate goal of justice, and law which cannot aspire to justice is, therefore, not worth administering.'[1]

Justice Delayed, Denied

In 1929, Mahatma Gandhi wrote in *Young India*, 'Whether Rama of my imagination ever lived or not on this earth, the ancient ideal of Ramarajya is undoubtedly one of true democracy in which the meanest citizen could be sure of swift justice without an elaborate and costly procedure. Even the dog is described by the poet to have received justice under Ramarajya.'

The founding fathers must have been familiar with the Gandhian conception of justice. Hence, the Preamble of the Indian Constitution promises its citizens a state committed to justice. The justice here is not narrow and not just legal justice.

Justice in the Constitution is all-encompassing–social, economic, and political. But have we fulfilled our constitutional guarantee?

Lord Yama is the God of death and justice, and it seems as if for an ordinary Indian citizen death is easier to be found than justice. This might seem an exaggeration and a bit far stretching of the metaphorical liberty, but it is not.

Umakant Mishra and Allah Singh, discussed in Chapter 1, are not aberrations but a norm. If we were to investigate, we would find thousands of cases where even simple judgments were not delivered before the death of the concerned parties, let alone a grand vision of justice.

According to the Economic Survey of 2018–19, it is not only the common person who fails to get judgments but also delays in contract enforcement and disposal resolution. These delays are arguably now the single biggest hurdle to the ease of doing business in India and higher gross domestic product (GDP) growth.

In 2019, Nitin Gadkari, the Union minister for road transport and highways, speaking at the ET CEO Roundtable, made a strong pitch for quick decisions by the judiciary. He said, 'I respect the Supreme Court, the judiciary. But in many cases, courts take a long time to deliver a verdict. Not taking a decision is a big problem and we know how courts take time. The delay in decision results in creating burden on agencies like NHAI to pay thousands of crores as compensation to contractors.'[2]

Despite repeated suggestions and remedies from various reports, commissions, and chief justices of India, we have not made sincere efforts to end the pathetic and insufferable court congestion. We have called for more judges, more courtrooms, more efficiency, and new judicial services, but nothing seems to be effective. However, this delay is not the inevitable fate of Indians but a remedial woo.

The Economic Survey of 2018–19 highlighted that the district and subordinate courts account for most of the pending cases in India, making them the priority for reform. Filling the vacant positions in the lower courts and high courts would enable them to dispose of all the cases (even without improving their productivity). A number of extra judges and an increase in the level of efficiency are also required to clear the backlog in five years. These targets are challenging but realistic. Four states, namely Uttar Pradesh, Bihar, Odisha, and West Bengal, deserve special attention. The number of working days for Indian courts is affected by the long and varied vacations they take. Different courts have different lengths of vacations, but they all reduce the time available for hearing cases. After deducting weekends and public holidays, the Supreme Court has 190 working days. This is lower than the average of 232 working days for high courts and 244 days for subordinate courts.

Heavy Cost of Justice

The newsletter of the International Institute for Conflict Prevention and Resolution by Elayne E. Greenberg and Noam Ebner includes a joke published in *The New Yorker*. The joke features a lawyer and a client sitting at a table while the lawyer evaluates the client's legal problem. 'You have a pretty good case,' the lawyer informs him, 'How much justice can you afford?'

Accessing justice in India is a serious problem for millions of people, especially the poor and marginalised, due to the high cost of litigation. Justice is a fundamental right and a prerequisite for the realisation of other rights and the achievement of peace, prosperity, and equanimity. However, the Indian justice system is plagued by the high cost of litigation that prevents people from seeking and obtaining justice. We have discussed the causes and consequences of the high cost of justice in India. Even the affluent and powerful are not immune to this problem, as seen in the case of a former coal secretary.

In 1956, the United States Supreme Court observed in the case of *Griffin vs Illinois*, 'There can be no equal justice where the kind of trial a man gets depends on the amount of money he has.'

This situation in India is worse. Senior lawyers charge lakhs of rupees for a case when some lawyers do not even get stipends. According to a report by *The Hindustan Times*, an undertrial prisoner, Abhishek alias Chhote Sarkar, was shot and killed inside the premises of the Danapur Civil Court Patna on December 15.[3] Revenge or gang rivalry might be the reason for such acts, but we forget that films often depict the protagonist taking justice in their hands when they fail to get justice because of high cost. In India, the client and the lawyer decide the fees that must be paid. The client being at the mercy of the lawyer is unaware of the actual cost.

The sky is the limit. It seems when it comes to lawyers' fees, it really is. In 2017, *The Hindustan Times* reported, 'What a lawyer charges a client remains largely unregulated in India. The advocates' fees rules are only for guidance and there is no bar to money claimed beyond what is fixed under the rules.'[4]

This situation is concerning and requires urgent action not only from the state but also from law firms and senior lawyers who have a leadership role in society. The Law Commission in its 131 Report titled *Role of Legal Profession in Administration of Justice* held,

> Monopoly is resented by the society because consumers of the monopoly can be held to ransom in the absence of availability of alternative services. A monopoly without a liability of accountability is likely to lead to tyranny. It is unquestionable that the legal profession is monopolistic in character. This does not

> need elaboration. If the profession is monopolistic in character, it must be accountable to the consumers of its services and let the consumer class be not narrowed down only to litigants. Even the court system of which it is an integral part can be said to be the consumer of its service. Therefore, apart from the wider concept of accountability of monopolistic profession to the society at large, there must be ways and means of making the legal profession accountable to the litigants and the court system.

We need to lead by example and allocate more funds towards legal services. We should also advocate for funding programmes that provide lawyers to low-income people in our communities. To further promote fairness and justice, we can also pass an act requiring all lawyers to take on pro bono cases. This might just make the system more just and fairer and transform the reality of a justice system that is blatantly elitist, favours the rich, excludes many people and may finally achieve justice for all.

Misuse of Law, Travesty of Justice

There has been a lot of discussion surrounding the misuse of law by the rich and powerful. It is not only the high cost of litigation but also the misuse of the law by the powerful individuals who burden the legal system with frivolous cases that drag on for years. They also misuse the law to intimidate the poor, vulnerable, and helpless.

Similarly, much has been written on how the state misuses the law either to stifle dissenting voices or to make its opponents fall in line. However, even when vulnerable sections abuse the due process to harass not-so-guilty people just to teach a lesson or for blackmailing and extortion, it is a problem.

The state has made many laws to ensure that there is not only equality before the law but also equal protection of the law. The intention was surely good, but the road to hell is paved with good intentions.

A legal provision should be made either in the existing law or a law that can be brought to deter the abuse of the law. This would not only save a lot of time, resources, and energy of the country's legal system, law enforcement, and other agencies but also help reduce the docket leading to an explosion-like situation.

Judicial Infrastructure

The Economic Survey of 2018–19 quotes a report by the National Institute of Public Finance and Policy, which states, 'For effective functioning, courts require competent administration to ensure that processes are followed, documents are submitted and stored, facilities are maintained, and human resources are managed. Court administration must support the judges in performing their core judicial functions efficiently.'

Courts in India lack not only judicial officers but also supporting infrastructure. Even if by a miracle or wishful thinking we could add more judges, it would be like getting a better-skilled driver to drive an old oil-guzzling, hard-clutched Ford Impala on an unpaved road and that too on a stormy and rainy night. Adequate facilities are the first and foremost requirement for ending the backlog and providing swift handling of cases.

Margaret Thatcher once said, 'You and I come by road or rail, but economists travel on infrastructure.' I do not know about economists, but justice surely does. We can take lessons and inspiration from other countries.

According to the information provided by Her Majesty's Courts and Tribunals Service (UK) website, the organisation offers supporting administration for fair, efficient, and accessible courts and tribunal systems. It works towards supporting an independent judiciary in the administration of justice, driving improvements across all aspects of the administration of the courts and tribunals, collaborating effectively with other justice organisations and agencies, including the legal professions, to improve access to justice, work with government departments and agencies to improve the quality and timeliness of their decision-making, which will reduce the number of cases coming before courts and tribunals.

In the USA, the Administrative Office of the U.S. Courts is the agency within the judicial branch that provides a broad range of legislative, legal, financial, technology, management, administrative, and programme support services to federal courts. A primary responsibility of the Administrative Office is to provide staff support and counsel to the judicial conference and its committees.

Along similar lines, a new service, named Indian Courts and Tribunal Services (ICTS), was proposed in the Economic Survey for India to handle the administrative matters of the legal system. The main functions of ICTS would be to

a) offer administrative assistance to the judiciary
b) detect and suggest improvements for process inefficiencies in the legal system, and
c) carry out the process of re-engineering.

The Hope: Alternative Dispute Redressal

According to a report by *The Print*, 'Overall, 57 central ministries and departments have 285,553 cases pending in high courts, district and sessions courts. In the past 10 years (2012–13 till 31 January 2023), the government incurred Rs 511.1 crore as litigation expense for payment of legal fees to government advocates/panel counsels in various courts and tribunals.'

The report further says, 'Non-performance of various wings of the executive and legislature has been cited as the reason for the government being the biggest litigants, accounting for nearly 50 per cent of the over 4 crore cases pending in various courts.'[5]

In 2017, the legal department urged government agencies to opt for online dispute resolution methods to expedite the settlement of conflicts and reduce the number of court cases involving the government, which make up almost half of the three crore cases that are still pending.[6]

The Indian judicial system has a vertical and pyramid-like structure. However, we need to explore horizontal solutions as well. After all, why should the 'Oceanic circle of Gandhi' not apply to the justice system?

Considering this, an alternative dispute resolution mechanism needs to be empowered because arbitration is supposed to be a swifter, quicker, cheaper, and more flexible way to resolve disputes, unlike the lengthy and formal procedures of litigation.

In the *Mumbai Kamgar Sabha, Bombay vs M/S Abdulbhai Faizullabhai 1976* case, Justice V. Krishnaiyer wrote that India is a developing country and needs techniques of maximising mediatory methodology as potent processes even where litigation has erupted. This is because there cannot be one but many roads leading to justice.

Legal Aid

The International Centre for Criminal Law Reform, in a report titled *Poverty and Access to Justice Review of the Literature* mentions, 'Poverty limits people's access to justice and their ability to resolve conflicts and deal with everyday legal problems. It is a very disempowering and alienating experience. The resulting inability to successfully resolve legal problems is itself contributing to people's inability to attain or maintain basic living standards. The justice system instead of empowering poor people and allowing them to fight for their rights is too often a source for them of frustration, disillusionment, and disempowerment, as well as a direct reflection of prevailing social inequality and exclusion.'[7]

Poverty not only births but also results in injustice. Supreme Court justice Sanjay Kishan Kaul once held that the 'poor who cannot afford lawyers remain in jails as undertrials while the rich get bail'.[8]

The Constitution of India, under Article 39A, specifically provides for the right to free legal aid to ensure that the poor and less fortunate also have access to justice. Hence came the Legal Services Authorities Act in 1987 (which came into force in 1995) to establish a nationwide uniform network to provide free and competent legal services to the weaker sections of society.

But the quality of legal aid is disappointing. During a lecture in Karnataka in 2022, former Supreme Court justice Uday U. Lalit said, 'Legal aid to the poor does not mean poor legal aid. There has to be better standard, better quality and better level.'[9]

We need to increase the quality of infrastructure, such as designated chambers for interacting with clients, increase the honorarium, and make sure that there is no delay in processing payments

Public Interest Litigation

In a court case regarding *Mumbai Kamgar Sabha, Bombay vs M/S Abdulbhai Faizullabhai* & *Ors* (10 March 1976), Justice V. Krishnaiyer stated that when there is no foul play and fairness is not faulted, allowing some flexibility in the legal process is a sign of justice. Legal proceedings such as test litigations, representative actions, pro bono publico are in line with the emphasis on justice for the common people and act as a deterrent for those who want to avoid confronting the real issues by relying on peripheral procedural shortcomings. PIL has been a significant tool for historically marginalised groups to seek justice. However, we need to examine whether the group for whom it was intended is using it and whether it is serving the purpose for which it was brought.

Conclusion

David Hume once said, 'To balance a large state of society whether monarchical or republican, on general laws, is a work of so great difficulty that no human genius however comprehensive, is able by the mere dint of reason and reflection, to effect it. The judgments of many should unite in this work; experience must guide their labour; time must bring it to perfection; and the feeling of inconvenience must correct the mistakes which they inevitably fall into in their first trials and experiments.'

This is especially true when it comes to ensuring that the promise of the social contract, which was signed in 1950, does not remain a cherished dream because of delays, high costs, misuse of law, and poor legal aid in the judiciary. In *S.P. Gupta vs President of India & Ors*, Justice P.N. Bhagwati on 30 December 1981, held, 'It is very easy for the human mind to find justification for a conclusion which accords with the dictates of emotion. Reason is a ready-enough advocate for the decision one, consciously or unconsciously, desires to reach. I will recall the brilliant fling of Shri Aurobindo in his poem "Savitri": "An inconclusive play is Reason's toil; Each strong idea can use her as its tool".'

For any reform, any change, and any amelioration we have to rid our minds of any preconceived notions. We will have to demand it. We will have to seek it. We will have to work on it. Because no messiah is coming to our aid with a magic wand wishing our problems away. After all *we* the people of India are the ultimate sovereign who solemnly resolved to secure to all its citizens: justice, social, economic and political, in other words, a Ram rajya.

Notes

Prologue

1 The Indian Express, 'Who Will Pay for Destroying 54 Years of This Man's Life?' *The Indian Express*, 14 October 2005, http://www.unipune.ac.in/snc/cssh/humanrights/01

2 The Times of India, 'Man in Jail for 54 Years Sans Trial, SC Issues Notice,' *The Times of India*, 11 October 2015, https://timesofindia.indiatimes.com/india/man-in-jail-for-54-years-sans-trial-sc-issues-notice/articleshow/1292611.cms

3 Constituent Assembly of India Debates (Proceedings) Volume 1, https://loksabha.nic.in/writereaddata/cadebatefiles/C17121946.html

4 The Indian Forum, 'The Curious Case of "Due Process" in the Indian Constitution,' *The Indian Forum*, 13 February 2023, https://www.theindiaforum.in/law/curious-case-due-process-indian-constitution

5 Zia Mody, *10 Judgements that Changed India* (New Delhi: Penguin, 41)

6 Durga Das Basu, *Introduction to the Constitution of India* (New Delhi: Lexis Nexis, 129-130)

7 Durga Das Basu, *Introduction to the Constitution of India*

8 Zia Mody, *10 Judgements that Changed India*

9 The Hindu, 'Justice Ramana Rues Unequal Access to Justice,' *The Hindu*, 23 March 2021, https://www.thehindu.com/news/national/justice-ramana-rues-unequal-access-to-justice/article34136153.ece

10 The Deccan Herald, 'Process Is the Punishment in Our Criminal Justice System: CJI Ramana.' *The Deccan Herald*, 16 July 2022, https://www.deccanherald.com/india/process-is-the-punishment-in-our-criminal-justice-system-cji-ramana-1127250.html#

Chapter 1: Justice Delayed, Denied

1 The Indian Express, 'With Verdict Family Left with No Hope,' *The Indian Express*, 25 August 2013, https://indianexpress.com/article/cities/chandigarh/with-verdict-family-left-with-no-hope/
2 The Indian Express, With Verdict Family Left with No Hope
3 The Indian Express, With Verdict Family Left with No Hope
4 The Indian Express, With Verdict Family Left with No Hope
5 The Hindustan Times, 'After 3 Decades of Trial and A Life Tainted By Murder Charge, Man Finally Acquitted,' *The Hindustan Times*, 11 February 2014, https://www.hindustantimes.com/chandigarh/after-3-decades-of-trial-and-a-life-tainted-by-murder-charge-man-finally-acquitted/story-U51WYwek5yVGIQQjRUVXEJ.html
6 ET Legal World, 'It May Take 500 Years to Dispose Of All Pending Cases,' *ET Legal World*, 4 August 2022, https://legal.economictimes.indiatimes.com/news/industry/it-may-take-500-years-to-dispose-off-all-pending-cases/93338563

Chapter 2: Heavy Cost of Justice

1 The Business Standard, 'High Cost of Litigation a Challenge Before Judiciary: Tewari,' *The Business Standard*, 24 October 2013, https://www.business-standard.com/article/current-affairs/high-cost-of-litigation-a-challenge-before-judiciary-tewari-113102400438_1.html
2 The Business Standard, 'High Cost of Litigation a Challenge Before Judiciary: Tewari.'
3 The Business Standard, 'High Cost of Litigation a Challenge Before Judiciary: Tewari.'
4 The Economic Times, 'Legal System Expensive, Big Lawyers Charge Like Taxis: Law Commission Chairman,' *The Economic Times*, 23 September 2017, https://economictimes.indiatimes.com/news/politics-and-nation/legal-system-expensive-big-lawyers-charge-like-taxis-law-commission-chairman/articleshow/60806645.cms
5 Daksh India, *Access to Justice Survey 2015*, https://dakshindia.org/wp-content/uploads/2016/05/Daksh-access-to-justice-survey.pdf
6 Address by the President of India Shri Ram Nath Kovind on the occasion of inaugurating the National Law Day Conference, 25 November 2017, https://ramnathkovind.nic.in/sp251117.html

7 Daksh India, *Access to Justice Survey 2015.*

8 The Times of India, 'Ram Jethmalani Bills Arvind Kejriwal Rs 3.42 Crore, Delhi Government Wants Taxpayers to Pay,' *The Times of India*, 4 April 2017, https://timesofindia.indiatimes.com/city/delhi/jethmalani-bills-cm-rs-3-42-crore-delhi-govt-wants-to-pick-up-tab/articleshow/57998275.cms

9 The Mint, 'How Much Do Delhi's Top Advocates Charge?' *The Mint*, 16 September 2015. https://www.livemint.com/Politics/BvOZE6z7Oyl6LiHZxWVlzL/How-much-do-Delhis-top-advocates-charge.html

10 Details available at https://www.legallyindia.com/the-bench-and-the-bar/revealed-delhi-rsquo-s-top-advocates-won-rsquo-t-even-touch-your-case-for-less-than-rs-5-lakh-20150908-6555

11 Details available at https://www.legallyindia.com/the-bench-and-the-bar/revealed-delhi-rsquo-s-top-advocates-won-rsquo-t-even-touch-your-case-for-less-than-rs-5-lakh-20150908-6555

12 Details available at https://main.sci.gov.in/sites/default/files/Supreme Court Rules, 2013.pdf

13 The Times of India, 'SC Asks Centre to Bring Law to Regulate Legal Profession, Cap Lawyers' Fees,' *The Times of India*, 6 December 2017, https://timesofindia.indiatimes.com/india/sc-asks-centre-to-bring-law-to-regulate-legal-profession-cap-lawyers-fees/articleshow/61939343.cms?from=mdr

14 The Times of India, 'SC Asks Centre to Bring Law to Regulate Legal Profession, Cap Lawyers' Fees.'

15 The Hindustan Times, 'Supreme Court Favours Law to Regulate Hefty Fees Charged By Lawyers,' *The Hindustan Times*, 7 December 2017, https://www.hindustantimes.com/india-news/sc-favours-law-to-regulate-hefty-fees-charged-by-lawyers/story-n1OdH52JcfVi5IPdwPgxvI.html

16 The Firstpost, 'Book Review: "Court on Trial": A Slim Read that Provides Comprehensive Assessment of Our Supreme Court,' The Firstpost, 27 August 2023, https://www.firstpost.com/opinion/book-review-court-on-trial-a-slim-read-that-provides-comprehensive-assessment-of-supreme-court-13045182.html

17 The Indian Express, 'No Tareekh Pe Tareekh Court: CJI Reiterates Views Against Repeated Case Adjournments,' *The Indian Express*, 4 November 2023, https://indianexpress.com/article/india/cji-chandrachud-dont-want-sc-to-become-tarikh-pe-tarikh-court-9011954/

18 The Indian Express, 'No Tareekh Pe Tareekh Court: CJI Reiterates Views Against Repeated Case Adjournments.'

Chapter 3: Misuse of Law, Travesty of Justice

1 Criminal Appeal No. 204 of 2021 (From Jail) (Defective Appeal No.386 of 2005), https://elegalix.allahabadhighcourt.in/elegalix/WebDownloadJudgmentDocument.do?judgmentID=8463686

2 The Times of India, 'Man, Wrongly Convicted by Trial Court, Is Set Free by High Court After Remaining in Jail for Two Decades,' *The Times of India*. 25 February 2021, https://timesofindia.indiatimes.com/city/kanpur/man-wrongly-convicted-by-trial-court-is-set-free-by-high-court-after-remaining-in-jail-for-two-decades/articleshow/81196169.cms

3 The Times of India, 'Man, Wrongly Convicted by Trial Court.'

4 Live Law, 'Allahabad HC Acquits Rape Accused in Jail for Over 19 Years, Raps Jail Authorities for Not Considering Case for Remission,' *Live Law*, 10 November 2022, https://www.livelaw.in/news-updates/allahabad-high-court-acquits-rape-accused-jail-over19years-raps-up-govt-not-considering-case-remission-213810

5 Case Title: *Nayan Prakash Singh @ Narayan Prakash Singh & Ors vs State of Jharkhand & Anr.* in the High Court of Jharkhand at Ranchi, Cr. M. P. No. 2596 of 2022

6 Case Title: *Rasik Lal Patel & Anr and State of Karnataka & Anr.* in the High Court of Karnataka at Bengaluru, 28 July 2023 [Criminal Petition No. 5497 of 2022]

7 Case Title: *Shamim and Others vs State of UP* [Criminal Appeal No. 5690 of 2004].

8 *Manak Chand @ Mani vs State of Haryana* [Criminal Appeal No. 2276 of 2014].

9 The Times of India, 'False Rape Cases a Travesty of Justice, Says Bombay High Court,' *The Times of India*. 29 February 2016, https://

timesofindia.indiatimes.com/city/mumbai/false-rape-cases-a-travesty-of-justice-says-bombay-high-court/articleshow/51182160.cms

Chapter 4: Infrastructure Woes

1 Amar Ujala, 'Gurugram District Court Building Collapsed,' *Amar Ujala*, 12 February 2022, https://www.amarujala.com/delhi-ncr/gurgaon/gurugram-district-court-building-collapsed

2 Dainik Jagran, 'अलीगढ़ में सीजेएम कोर्ट की बिल्डिंग का एक हिस्सा गिरा, वकील घायल,' *Dainik Jagran*, 22 July 2020, https://www.jagran.com/uttar-pradesh/aligarh-city-a-part-of-cjm-court-building-collapsed-in-aligarh-lawyer-injured-20540767.html

3 Live Law, ''No Infrastructure Project Getting Cleared, Funds Not Being Released': High Court to Delhi Govt on Lack of Space in District Courts,' *Live Law*, 1 December 2023, https://www.livelaw.in/high-court/delhi-high-court/delhi-high-court-uncleared-infrastructure-projects-funds-delhi-government-district-courts-243470#:~:text=The Delhi High Court on,District Courts in the city.

4 Live Law, 'No Infrastructure Project Getting Cleared.'

5 The Business Standard, 'SC Seeks Centre's Stand on Plea Regarding Judicial Vista Construction,' *The Business Standard*, 25 April 2022, https://www.business-standard.com/article/current-affairs/sc-seeks-centre-s-stand-on-plea-regarding-judicial-vista-construction-122042500623_1.html

6 Live Law, 'National Company Law Tribunals; Reeling Under Poor Infrastructure,' *Live Law*, 1 April 2022, https://www.livelaw.in/columns/national-company-law-tribunals-nclt-companies-act-2013-insolvency-and-bankruptcy-code-195594

7 The Indian Express, 'Bombay HC Pulls Up State Govt, Questions Taking 16 Years to Find Space for MSHRC,' *The Indian Express*, 1 August 2017. https://indianexpress.com/article/cities/mumbai/bombay-hc-pulls-up-state-govt-questions-taking-16-years-to-find-space-for-mshrc-4776506/

8 *Sales Tax Tribunal Bar Association and Another Vs the State of Maharashtra and Others*. Writ Petition Number 2069 of 2015.

9 Press Information Bureau, 'Cabinet Approves Continuation of the Centrally Sponsored Scheme (CSS) for Development of Infrastructure Facilities for Judiciary for Further Five Years,' *Press Information Bureau*, July 14, 2021. https://pib.gov.in/PressReleasePage.aspx?PRID=1735375

10 The Print, 'What is NJIC? Agency to Monitor Infrastructure Development in Trial Courts, Proposed by CJI,' *The Print*, 23 September 2021, https://theprint.in/judiciary/what-is-njic-agency-to-monitor-infrastructure-development-in-trial-courts-proposed-by-cji/738593/

11 The Times of India, 'Judicial Infrastructure: 21k Court Halls Now Available: Government to House,' *The Times of India*, 4 August 2023.

12 The Print, 'What is NJIC? Agency to Monitor Infrastructure Development in Trial Courts, Proposed by CJI,' *The Print*, 23 September 2021, https://theprint.in/judiciary/what-is-njic-agency-to-monitor-infrastructure-development-in-trial-courts-proposed-by-cji/738593/

13 Since the inception of the scheme till 2014, the Central Government over 20 years provided only Rs 3444 crore to the state governments/union territories. In sharp contrast, the present government during first seven years sanctioned Rs 5200 crore till date accounting for nearly 60 per cent of the sanction made till 2021.

14 Vidhi, 'Budgeting Better for Courts-An Evaluation of the Rs 7460 Crores Released Under the Centrally Sponsored Scheme for Judicial Infrastructure,' *Vidhi*, 3 September 2019, https://vidhilegalpolicy.in/research/budgeting-better-for-courts-an-evaluation-of-the-rs-7460-crores-released-under-the-centrally-sponsored-scheme-for-judicial-infrastructure/

15 Vidhi, 'Budgeting Better for Courts.'

16 Nikhil Majithia, 'What's Stopping India's Judicial Infrastructure Upgrade? The Absence of Centre-State Unity,' *The Print*, 21 December 2022.

17 The Hindu, 'Inadequate Judicial Infrastructure, Vacancies Are Reasons for Pending Court Cases, Says Former CJI,' *The Hindu*, 24 January 2023, https://www.thehindu.com/news/cities/chennai/

inadequate-judicial-infrastructure-vacancies-are-reasons-for-pending-court-cases-says-former-cji/article66427843.ece

18 The Hindu, 'Judicial Infrastructure, A Neglected Case,' *The Hindu*, 6 December 2021, https://www.thehindu.com/news/cities/Delhi/judicial-infrastructure-a-neglected-case/article37859686.ece#

19 The Hindu, 'With Kiren Rijiju Listening, CJI N V Ramana Rues Poor Judicial Infrastructure,' *The Hindu*, 24 October 2021, https://www.newindianexpress.com/thesundaystandard/2021/oct/24/with-kiren-rijiju-listening-cji-n-v-ramana-rues-poor-judicial-infrastructure-2374936.html

20 Press Information Bureau, 'Strength of Judges. Ministry of Law and Justice,' *Press Information Bureau,* 24 March 2023, https://pib.gov.in/PressReleasePage.aspx?PRID=1910433#:~:text=Strength of Judges, 37 24more rows

21 Centre for Research and Planning, *Subordinate Courts of India: A Report on Access to Justice 2016* (New Delhi: Centre for Research and Planning, 2016), https://main.sci.gov.in/pdf/AccesstoJustice/Subordinate%20Court%20of%20India.pdf

22 Live Law, '26% of Court Complexes in India Don't Have Separate Ladies' Toilets: Union Law Minister Informs Rajyasabha,' *Live Law*, 20 December 2022, https://www.livelaw.in/news-updates/union-law-minister-kiren-rijiju-informs-rajyasabha-separate-ladies-toilets-court-complexes-217171

23 Live Law, '26% of Court Complexes in India Don't Have Separate Ladies.'

24 *All India Judges Association and Ors vs Union of India (UoI) and Ors* on 8 February 2001, https://indiankanoon.org/doc/1245776/

25 The Indian Express, 'Demand for 40,000 Judges Not Backed by Data: Law Minister,' *The Indian Express*, 26 May 2016, https://indianexpress.com/article/india/india-news-india/demand-for-40000-judges-not-backed-by-data-law-minister-v-sadananda-gowda-2819405/

26 The Indian Express, 'Fewer Judges Increasing Pendency, Hope for Movement by Govt to Clear Names: CJI,' *The Indian Express*, 5 July 2022.

27 The Times of India, 'It'll Take 320 Years to Clear Legal Backlog.' *The Times of India,* 7 March 2010, https://timesofindia.indiatimes.com/india/itll-take-320-years-to-clear-legal-backlog/articleshow/5652826.cms

28 Law Beat, 'Environment of Some District Courts Such That Lady Advocates Feel Apprehensive About Entering Court Room: CJI Calls for Inclusive Infrastructure,' *Law Beat*, 30 April 2022, https://lawbeat.in/top-stories/environment-some-district-courts-such-lady-advocates-feel-apprehensive-about-entering

29 Press Information Bureau, 'National Judicial Infrastructure Authority of India.' *Press Information Bureau*, 21 March 2022, https://www.pib.gov.in/PressReleasePage.aspx?PRID=1807611

30 The Economic Times, 'CJI Rues Lack of Basic Judicial Infra, Stresses Need of Filling Vacancies, Raising No. of Judges,' *The Economic Times*, 26 February 2022, https://economictimes.indiatimes.com/news/india/cji-rues-lack-of-basic-judicial-infra-stresses-need-of-filling-vacancies-raising-no-of-judges/articleshow/89847830.cms

31 Lok Sabha, 'Unstarred Question No 3363,' 5 August 2022, https://cdnbbsr.s3waas.gov.in/s35d6646aad9bcc0be55b2c82f69750387/uploads/2022/11/2022110976.pdf

32 Press Information Bureau, 'Cabinet Approves eCourts Phase III for 4 Years,' *Press Information Bureau,* September 13, 2023. https://pib.gov.in/PressReleaseIframePage.aspx?PRID=1956919

33 Press Information Bureau, 'Status of f eCOURTS mission mode project (MMP).' *Press Information Bureau,* August 3, 2023. https://pib.gov.in/PressReleaseIframePage.aspx?PRID=1945462

Chapter 5: Right to Legal Aid

1 Live Law, "Guarantee of Equal Justice Meaningless If Vulnerable Sections Cannot Enforce Their Rights Because of Poverty, Illiteracy or Weakness': Justice NV Ramana,' *Live Law*, 23 March 2021, https://www.livelaw.in/news-updates/guarantee-of-equal-justice-meaningless-if-vulnerable-sections-cannot-enforce-their-rights-because-of-poverty-illiteracy-or-weakness-justice-nv-ramana-171568

2 National Legal Services Authority (NALSA), https://doj.gov.in/access-to-justice-for-the-marginalized/

3 Access to Justice Survey-Daksh India, https://www.dakshindia.org/access-to-justice-survey/

4 The Hindu, 'Legal Aid to the Poor Does Not Mean Poor Legal Aid: Justice Lalit,' *The Hindu*, 24 October 2021, https://www.thehindu.com/news/national/karnataka/legal-aid-to-the-poor-does-not-mean-poor-legal-aid-justice-lalit/article37148448.ece

5 India Justice Report, *India Justice Report: Ranking States on Police, Judiciary, Prisons and Legal Aid* (New Delhi: India Justice Report, 2022)

6 India Justice Report, *India Justice Report 2022*.

7 IndiaSpend, 'Low Payments, Lack of Respect: Why Quality of Free Legal Aid in India's Districts Is Poor,' *IndiaSpend*, 19 December 2022

8 Press Information Bureau, 'Legal Aid to Poor and Marginalized Sections,' *Press Information Bureau*. 23 March 2023, https://pib.gov.in/Pressreleaseshare.aspx?PRID=1910032

9 The Economic Times, 'Litigation Is Like Bleeding Wound, Says CJI-Designate Justice Uday Umesh Lalit; Wants Free Legal Aid for Poor,' *The Economic Times*, 21 August 2022, https://economictimes.indiatimes.com/news/india/litigation-is-like-bleeding-wound-says-cji-designate-justice-uday-umesh-lalit-wants-free-legal-aid-for-poor/articleshow/93694588.cms

10 The Economic Times, 'Litigation Is Like Bleeding Wound.'

11 Legal Aid Defense Counsel Scheme 2022, https://drive.google.com/file/d/1cbWZq7aD3IWMRHOu8AvxUkXJQKO_LYP-/view

Chapter 6: Public Interest Litigation

1 Status Note on Police Reforms in India, https://www.mha.gov.in/sites/default/files/PoliceReforms(E)181013.pdf

2 The India Today, 'Women's Group Shaken after Jaipur Court Dismisses Bhanwari Devi Rape Case and Clears Accused,' *The India Today*, 15 December 1995, https://www.indiatoday.in/magazine/special-report/story/19951215-womens-group-shaken-after-jaipur-court-dismisses-bhanwari-devi-rape-case-and-clears-accused-808044-1995-12-14

3 Zia Mody, *10 Judgments That Changed India* (New Delhi: Penguin, 2013)

4 These lines are by Senior Advocate Shyam Divan in Sujit Choudhry, Madhav Khosla, and Pratap Bhanu Mehta (eds), 'Public Interest Litigation', *Oxford Handbook of the Indian Constitution* (Oxford: Oxford University Press, 2016)

5 The Firstpost, 'Soli Sorabjee on PILs: Every Matter of Public Interest Cannot Be a Matter of Public Interest Litigation,' The Firstpost, 21 January 2016, https://www.firstpost.com/india/soli-sorabjee-on-pils-every-matter-of-public-interest-cannot-be-a-matter-of-public-interest-litigation-2592886.html

Chapter 7: The Hope: Alternative Dispute Redressal

1 Press Information Bureau, 'Approachable Judicial System to Common Man,' *Press Information Bureau*, 4 August 2023, https://pib.gov.in/PressReleasePage.aspx?PRID=1945771

2 The Hindu, '63-year-old Civil Dispute Pending in Hubballi Court Among Oldest Cases Settled in Lok Adalat,' *The Hindu*, 10 July 2023, https://www.thehindu.com/news/national/karnataka/63-year-old-civil-dispute-pending-in-hubballi-court-among-oldest-cases-settled-in-lok-adalat/article67064285.ece#

3 Press Information Bureau, 'The Lok Adalat Is One of the Important Alternative Disputes Resolution (ADR) Mechanism Available to Common People,' *Press Information Bureau*, 16 December 2022, PressReleaseIframePage.aspx

4 The Hindu, 'Odisha Man Sues Modi After Failing to Get Aadhaar Card Despite 21 Attempts,' *The Hindu*, 24 September 2022, https://www.thehindu.com/news/national/other-states/odisha-man-sues-modi-after-failing-to-get-aadhaar-card-despite-21-attempts/article32683655.ece

5 The Hindu, 'For Lok Adalats, Speed Overrides Quality,' *The Hindu*, 7 April 2021, https://www.thehindu.com/opinion/op-ed/for-lok-adalats-speed-overrides-quality/article34267191.ece

Conclusion

1 *Samarpal & Ors vs UoIi & Ors.* Judgment Date: July 4, 2022, http://164.100.69.66/jsearch/

2 The Times of India, 'Delay in Court Decisions Hurts Govt Financially, Says Nitin Gadkari,' *The Times of India*, 26 September 2019, https://

timesofindia.indiatimes.com/india/delay-in-court-decisions-hurts-govt-financially-says-nitin-gadkari/articleshow/71302965.cms

3 The Hindustan Times, 'Bihar: Undertrial Prisoner Shot Dead Inside Danapur Court Premises; Two Held,' *The Hindustan Times*, 15 December 2023, https://www.hindustantimes.com/cities/others/bihar-undertrial-prisoner-shot-dead-inside-danapur-court-premises-two-held-101702641940965.html

4 The Hindustan Times, 'Supreme Court Favours Law to Regulate Hefty Fees Charged by Lawyers,' *The Hindustan Times*, 7 December 2017, https://www.hindustantimes.com/india-news/sc-favours-law-to-regulate-hefty-fees-charged-by-lawyers/story-n1OdH52JcfVi5IPdwPgxvI.html

5 The Print, 'Central Ministries Biggest Litigants in Govt with 2.85 Lakh Pending Cases, Finance Tops List,' *The Print*, 27 February 2023, https://theprint.in/judiciary/central-ministries-biggest-litigants-in-govt-with-2-85-lakh-pending-cases-finance-tops-list/1400586/

6 The Times of India, 'Govt Departments Told to Go for e-arbitration to Speed Up Dispute Resolution,' *The Times of India*, 21 August 2017, https://timesofindia.indiatimes.com/india/govt-deptartments-told-to-go-for-e-arbitration-to-speed-up-dispute-resolution/articleshow/60150587.cms

7 International Centre for Criminal Law Reform, *Poverty and Access to Justice* (Vancouver: International Centre for Criminal Law Reform, 2022), https://icclr.org/wp-content/uploads/2022/02/Access-to-Justice-and-Poverty_ICCLR_RR-2022-2_Bellsmith-Goertzen-Neilsen-Stinson.pdf

8 Bar and Bench, 'Poor Who Cannot Afford Lawyers Remain in Jails as Undertrials While Rich Get Bail: Supreme Court Justice Sanjay Kishan Kaul,' *Bar and Bench*, 19 September 2023, https://www.barandbench.com/news/trend-undertrial-prisoners-disturbing-supreme-court-justice-sanjay-kishan-kaul-2023

9 The Hindu, 'Legal Aid to the Poor Does Not Mean Poor Legal Aid: Justice Lalit,' *The Hindu*, 24 October 2021, https://www.thehindu.com/news/national/karnataka/legal-aid-to-the-poor-does-not-mean-poor-legal-aid-justice-lalit/article37148448.ece

References

Amar Ujala. 'Gurugram district court building collapsed.' *Amar Ujala.* 12 February 2022.

Bar and Bench. 'Poor who cannot afford lawyers remain in jails as undertrials while rich get bail: Supreme Court Justice Sanjay Kishan Kaul.' *Bar and Bench.* 19 September 2023.

Basu, Durga Das. *Introduction to the Constitution of India.* New Delhi: Lexis Nexis, 2022.

Daksh India. *Access to Justice Survey 2015.*

ET Legal World. 'It may take 500 years to dispose of all pending cases.' *ET Legal World.* 4 August 2022.

Firstpost. 'Soli Sorabjee on PILs: Every matter of public interest cannot be a matter of public interest litigation.' Firstpost. 21 January 2016.

Firstpost. 'Book Review: "Court on Trial": A slim read that provides comprehensive assessment of our Supreme Court.' Firstpost. 27 August 2023.

IndiaSpend. 'Low payments, lack of respect: why quality of free legal aid In India's districts is poor.' *IndiaSpend.*19 December 2022.

India Today. 'Women's group shaken after Jaipur court dismisses Bhanwari Devi rape case and clears accused.' *India Today.* 15 December 1995.

International Centre for Criminal Law Reform. *Poverty and Access to Justice.* 3 February 2022.

Law Beat. 'Environment of some district courts such that lady advocates feel apprehensive about entering court room: CJI calls for inclusive infrastructure.' *Law Beat.* 30 April 2022.

Live Law. 'National company law tribunals; reeling under poor infrastructure.' *Live Law.* 1 April 2022.

Live Law. 'Allahabad HC acquits rape accused in jail for over 19 yrs, raps jail authorities for not considering case for remission.' *Live Law*. 10 November 2022.

Live Law. '26% of court complexes in India don't have separate ladies' toilets: union law minister informs Rajyasabha.' *Live Law*. 20 December 2022.

Live Law. '"No infrastructure project getting cleared, funds not being released": high court to Delhi govt on lack of space in district courts.' *Live Law*. 1 December 2023.

Live Law. '"Guarantee of equal justice meaningless if vulnerable sections cannot enforce their rights because of poverty, illiteracy or weakness": Justice NV Ramana.' *Live Law*. 23 March 2021.

Majithia, Nikhil. 'What's stopping India's judicial infrastructure upgrade? The absence of Centre-state unity.' *The Print*. 21 December 2022.

Mody, Zia. *10 Judgements that Changed India*. New Delhi: Penguin, 2013.

Press Information Bureau. 'Cabinet approves continuation of the Centrally Sponsored Scheme (CSS) for Development of Infrastructure Facilities for Judiciary for further five years.' *Press Information Bureau*. 14 July 2021._

Press Information Bureau. 'National Judicial Infrastructure Authority of India.' *Press Information Bureau*. 21 March 2022._

Press Information Bureau. 'The lok adalat is one of the important Alternative Disputes Resolution (ADR) mechanism available to common people.' *Press Information Bureau*. 16 December 2022. PressReleaseIframePage.aspx

Press Information Bureau. 'Legal aid to poor and marginalized sections.' *Press Information Bureau*. 23 March 2023.

Press Information Bureau. 'Approachable judicial system to common man.' *Press Information Bureau*. 4 August 2023.

Press Information Bureau, 'Status of ecourts mission mode project (MMP).' *Press Information Bureau,* 3 August 2023.

Press Information Bureau. 'Cabinet approves ecourts phase III for 4 years.' *Press Information Bureau*. 13 September 2023._

The Business Standard. 'High cost of litigation a challenge before judiciary: Tewari.' *The Business Standard*. 24 October 2013.

The Business Standard. 'SC seeks Centre's stand on plea regarding Judicial Vista construction.' *The Business Standard*. 25 April 2022.

The Deccan Herald. 'Process is the punishment in our criminal justice system: CJI Ramana.' *The Deccan Herald*. 16 July 2022.

The Economic Times. 'Legal system expensive, big lawyers charge like taxis: Law Commission chairman.' *The Economic Times*. 23 September 2017.

The Economic Times. 'CJI rues lack of basic judicial infra, stresses need of filling vacancies, raising no. of judges.' *The Economic Times*. 26 February 2022.

The Economic Times. 'Litigation is like bleeding wound, says CJI-designate Justice Uday Umesh Lalit; wants free legal aid for poor.' *The Economic Times*. 21 August 2022.

The Hindu. 'Justice Ramana rues unequal access to justice.' *The Hindu*. 23 March 2021.

The Hindu. 'For Lok Adalats, speed overrides quality'. *The Hindu*. 07 April 2021.

The Hindu. 'Legal aid to the poor does not mean poor legal aid: Justice Lalit.'. *The Hindu*. 24 October 2021.

The Hindu. 'With Kiren Rijiju listening, CJI N V Ramana rues poor judicial infrastructure.' *The Hindu*. 24 October 2021.

The Hindu. 'Judicial infrastructure, a neglected case.' *The Hindu*. 06 December 2021.

The Hindu. 'Odisha man sues Modi after failing to get Aadhaar card despite 21 attempts.' *The Hindu*. 24 September 2022.

The Hindu. 'Inadequate judicial infrastructure, vacancies are reasons for pending court cases, says former CJI.' *The Hindu*. 24 January 2023.

The Hindu. '63-year-old civil dispute pending in Hubballi court among oldest cases settled in Lok Adalat.' *The Hindu*. 10 July 2023.

The Hindustan Times. 'After 3 decades of trial and a life tainted by murder charge, man finally acquitted.' *The Hindustan Times*. 11 February 2014.

The Hindustan Times. 'Supreme Court favours law to regulate hefty fees charged by lawyers.' *The Hindustan Times*. 7 December 2017.

The Hindustan Times. "Bihar: Undertrial prisoner shot dead inside Danapur court premises; two held". *The Hindustan Times.* 15 December 2023.

The Indian Express. 'Who will pay for destroying 54 years of this man's life?' *The Indian Express.* 14 October 2005.

The Indian Express. 'With verdict family left with no hope.' *The Indian Express.* 25 August 2013.

The Indian Express. 'Demand for 40,000 judges not backed by data: Law minister.' *The Indian Express.* 26 May 2016.

The Indian Express. 'Bombay HC pulls up state govt, questions taking 16 years to find space for MSHRC.' *The Indian Express.* 1 August 2017.

The Indian Express. 'Fewer judges increasing pendency, hope for movement by govt to clear names: CJI.' *The Indian Express.* 5 July 2022.

The Indian Express. 'No tareekh pe tareekh court: CJI reiterates views against repeated case adjournments.' *The Indian Express.* 4 November 2023.

The Indian Forum. 'The curious case of 'due process' in the Indian Constitution.' *The Indian Forum.* 13 February 2023.

The Mint. 'How much do Delhi's top advocates charge?' *The Mint.* 16 September 2015.

The Print. 'What is NJIC? Agency to monitor infrastructure development in trial courts, proposed by CJI.' *The Print.* 23 September 2021.

The Print. 'Central ministries biggest litigants in govt with 2.85 lakh pending cases, finance tops list.' *The Print.* 27 February 2023.

The Times of India. 'It'll take 320 years to clear legal backlog.' *The Times of India.* 7 March 2010.

The Times of India. 'Man in jail for 54 years sans trial, SC issues notice.' *The Times of India.* 11 October 2015.

The Times of India. 'False rape cases a travesty of justice, says Bombay high court.' *The Times of India.* 29 February 2016.

The Times of India. 'Ram Jethmalani bills Arvind Kejriwal Rs 3.42 crore, Delhi government wants taxpayers to pay.' *The Times of India.* 4 April 2017.

The Times of India. 'Govt departments told to go for e-arbitration to speed up dispute resolution.' *The Times of India*. 21 August 2017.

The Times of India. 'Delay in court decisions hurts govt financially, says Nitin Gadkari.' *The Times of India.* 26 September 2019.

The Times of India. 'Man, wrongly convicted by trial court, is set free by high court after remaining in jail for two decades.' *The Times of India*. 25 February 2021.

The Times of India. 'Judicial infrastructure: 21k court halls now available: government to house.' *The Times of India*. 4 August 2023.

Vidhi. 'Budgeting better for courts-an evaluation of the Rs 7460 crores released under the Centrally Sponsored Scheme for Judicial Infrastructure.' *Vidhi.* 3 September 2019.

About the Author

Shishir Tripathi is a freelance journalist and researcher based in Delhi and writes for News18.com and Firstpost. He has worked at *The Indian Express*, Firstpost, *GovernanceNow*, and Indic Collective. While at *The Indian Express* and Firstpost, he covered the courts, and for over a decade now, he has been writing on legal issues. *Stalled Wheels of Justice* is his first foray into writing a book.